TRAEGER GRILL BIBLE 2025

LIAM WALKER

YOUR FREE GIFTS

Ready to unlock the full potential of your Traeger grill? We have something exciting just for you!

Scan the QR code provided and gain exclusive access to three meticulously curated guides Traeger Chef Secret, Pairing Food with Events and Beverages, and Around the World with Your Trager. Each guide if filled with insights to enhance your grilling skills and culinary adventures

Ready to elevate your grilling game? Scan now to explore these free resources and discover the incredible benefits of mastering your Traege grill!

SCAN THE QR CODE BELOW TO DOWNLOAD YOUR FREE GIFTS

TABLE OF CONTENTS

INTRODUCTION

WELCOME TO THE WORLD OF TRAEGER GRILLING

Hello, and congratulations on taking the first step towards mastering the art of Traeger grilling! Whether you've just unboxed your brand-new Traeger grill or you've been tentatively trying out a few recipes, you're in the right place. This book is designed not just to guide you through the myriad of delicious possibilities your Traeger grill offers, but also to transform the way you cook and entertain.

Grilling with a Traeger is more than just cooking; it's about experiencing the joy of creating mouthwatering dishes with ease. A Traeger isn't just any grill—it uses wood pellets and unique heating system to infuse your food with rich, smoky flavors that can't be achieved with traditional charcoal or gas grills. From smoky briskets to crisp vegetables, your Traeger is versatile enough to handle it all.

As we proceed, I'll share everything I've learned from my years of grilling—mistakes to avoid, tips for success, and some of my all-time favorite recipes. This isn't just about following steps; it's about understanding your grill's potential to make every meal memorable.

WHAT TO EXPECT FROM THIS BOOK

This book is crafted to be your ultimate guide to mastering the Traeger grill. It's structured to walk you through every aspect of Traeger grilling, starting with the basics of setting up your grill and understanding how it works. From there, we'll explore a wide variety of recipes—over 100 to be precise—that will expand your culinary skills and impress not just your family but any guest that might join your table.

Each chapter is designed to build on the previous one, gradually increasing in complexity as your confidence and skills grow. You'll learn how to cook different types of meats, fish and vegetables and get creative with desserts. I've also included chapters dedicated to maintenance tips to keep your Traeger in top shape, ensuring years of enjoyable grilling. I've made sure that the instructions are clear and straightforward, devoid of unnecessary jargon, making each step easy to follow. You won't find long lists of dos and don'ts. Instead, you'll encounter advice and insights shared as if I were right there beside you, talking you through each process.

Let's start with setting up your grill. If you've just bought your Traeger, the excitement of unpacking it is something most grill enthusiasts remember for a long time. The setup process is straightforward. Ensure you're placing your grill on a flat, stable surface away from any combustible materials. Once set, it's important to 'season' your grill before the first use, which involves running it at a high temperature for a few hours to burn off any residue from the manufacturing process. This not only cleans your grill but also primes for optimal performance.

Understanding the fuel for your Traeger—wood pellets—is crucial. These aren't just any wood chips; they come in various flavors like hickory, apple, cherry, and mesquite, each adding a distinct profile to your food. Matching the correct wood pellet with the right food can elevate your dish from good to extraordinary. For instance, apple pellets work wonders with pork and poultry, imparting a mild, sweet smokiness that enhances the meat's natural flavors.

Your Traeger grill is incredibly versatile. It allows you to grill, smoke, roast, braise, and even bake. Each cooking method can be adapted to suit whatever dish you're preparing. Smoking a brisket at a low temperature for several hours allows it to absorb the smoky flavor deeply, resulting in tender, flavorful meat that pulls apart with just the tug of a fork. Grilling, on the other hand, is perfect for those sear marks and crisp edges that make a steak or a burger irresistibly appetizing.

Through this book, expect to find not just a collection of recipes, but a new way to think about cooking and entertaining. It's about making the most of your Traeger grill and enjoying the process as much as the delicious results. So, fire up your grill, gather your ingredients, and let's get grilling!

CHAPTER 1: MASTERING YOUR TRAEGER GRILL

UNDERSTANDING YOUR TRAEGER GRILL

Welcome to the world of Traeger grilling, where the aroma of smoked meats and the warmth of the grill make any backyard the place to be. Your new Traeger grill isn't just another cooking appliance; it's a gateway to a new way of preparing food that combines simplicity with versatility. Let's begin by demystifying what makes a Traeger grill a favorite among both novices and seasoned grill masters.

A Traeger grill operates on wood pellets and is powered by electricity. This unique combination allows for precise temperature control, which is crucial for both low-and-slow cooking and hot-and-fast grilling. What sets it apart is its ability to maintain steady temperatures without the constant need to adjust the heat manually. This consistency is achieved through an automated auger that feeds pellets into the firepot where they are ignited, maintaining the temperature you've set so you can focus more on your guests and less on the grill.

The smoke produced by the burning of wood pellets is what gives Traeger-cooked foods their distinct flavor. Unlike charcoal grills, the smoke from a Traeger is milder and more controlled, allowing the natural flavors of the food to shine through while still imparting the smoky taste that barbecue enthusiasts love. Whether you're preparing a tender piece of fish, a hearty brisket, or even baking a pizza, the Traeger does it all with a flavor profile that can only be described as out-of-this-world.

Traeger grills are designed for ease of use, featuring electronic start and temperature control systems that make grilling almost as easy as cooking in your kitchen. The digital controller manages the internal temperature by adjusting the pellet feed rate and airflow, ensuring that you can step away from the grill without fear of major temperature swings.

One of the joys of cooking with a Traeger is the versatility it offers. Not limited to just grilling and smoking, these grills are capable of baking, roasting, braising, and barbecuing, providing a wide array of cooking options. Imagine baking a loaf of artisan bread on the grill or even roasting a Thanksgiving turkey. The possibilities are nearly endless, making it a must-have tool for any culinary enthusiast.

The key to unlocking the full potential of your Traeger lies in understanding the various wood pellets you can use. Each type of wood pellet offers a different flavor, from the strong, bold notes of mesquite to the sweet, subtle undertones of applewood. Choosing the right pellet can enhance the taste of your dishes, turning simple meals into exquisite culinary creations.

For those who love experimenting, the Traeger grill is a playground. You can mix different types of wood pellets to create custom flavor profiles, perfectly matching the wood smoke with the ingredients and recipes you're using. This kind of customization is what makes Traeger grilling a truly personal cooking experience.

In addition to the culinary versatility, the Traeger grill is incredibly efficient. The pellets are made from compressed hardwood sawdust and burn cleanly and efficiently, producing very little ash compared to charcoal. This means less cleanup and more environmentally friendly cooking, aligning with the preferences of those who prioritize sustainability in their cooking practices.

Moreover, the Traeger grill's design includes features that cater to the modern cook. Many models are equipped with Wi-Fi capabilities, allowing you to control the grill via a smartphone app. This smart technology means you can monitor the temperature, adjust the smoke level, and even receive alerts about your food, all from the comfort of your chair.

Remember that, like any method of cooking, it comes with a learning curve. The first few times you use your grill, take it as an opportunity to experiment with temperatures and cooking times, as well as the different flavors of pellets. Keep a journal of your attempts, noting what works and what doesn't, and you'll soon master the art of Traeger grilling.

Finally, remember that maintenance is key to your Traeger's longevity and performance. Regularly cleaning the grill, especially the grease drain system and the firepot, ensures it remains in top working order and ready for your next grilling session. With proper care, your Traeger grill will serve as the centerpiece of countless enjoyable meals and gatherings.

There's something extraordinary about the way food tastes when it's prepared on a Traeger, and with each meal, you'll grow more confident and creative in your grilling. Welcome to the satisfying, flavorful world of Traeger grilling — let the feasts begin!

ESSENTIAL TOOLS AND ACCESSORIES

To fully enjoy and extend the capabilities of your Traeger grill, complementing it with the right tools and accessories is vital. While your Traeger is designed to handle a variety of grilling tasks right out of the box, a few carefully chosen additions can significantly enhance your cooking experience. Let's explore some indispensable items that will make your grilling smoother and more enjoyable.

PELLET STORAGE

Wood pellets are the heart of your Traeger grill, fueling it to create those wonderful smoky flavors. It is imperative to store them correctly to maintain their quality. Moisture is the enemy here; it can cause the pellets to swell, disintegrate, and potentially clog the auger system, leading to a malfunction. To prevent such issues, invest in a high-quality, airtight storage container. These containers are designed to keep your pellets dry and fresh, ready for your next grilling session. Place it in a cool, dry area away from direct sunlight to preserve the integrity of the pellets.

MEAT PROBES

Most Traeger grills come equipped with at least one meat probe, but having a spare can b
a game-changer, especially when cooking multiple types of meat or large cuts that migh
require different cooking times. These probes help you monitor the internal temperatur
of your meats without opening the grill lid, which can cause significant heat loss and exten
cooking times. By ensuring that you're cooking your meat to the perfect temperature, yo
can achieve consistent, mouth-watering results every time.

GRILL COVERS

Protecting your Traeger grill from the elements is crucial, especially if you keep it outdoor
Exposure to rain, snow, or even too much sun can wear down your grill over time. A high
quality grill cover that fits your model snugly can shield your grill from weather-relate
damage, keep it clean, and extend its lifespan. Ensure the cover is made from durable
waterproof material and fits tightly around the grill to prevent any water from seeping ir

GRILLING UTENSILS

The right set of grilling utensils will enhance your safety and ease of cooking. A long
handled spatula, tongs, and a meat fork are essential for handling food safely withou
getting too close to the heat. Look for utensils made from high-quality, durable material
like stainless steel that can withstand high temperatures and are easy to clean. Som
utensils come with rubber or silicone handles, which provide a comfortable, non-slip grip

CLEANING SUPPLIES

Keeping your Traeger clean is not just about maintenance; it's about ensuring the qualit
and safety of the food you cook. Regular cleaning prevents buildup from grease and foo
particles, which can cause flare-ups or smoke that might impart a bitter flavor to you
dishes. Use a grill brush to scrub the grates after each use, and employ cleaners designe
specifically for grills to keep the exterior shiny and deposit-free. Also, make sure t
regularly empty and clean the drip tray and replace the liners to maintain a clean an
fire-safe grilling environment.

ADDITIONAL HANDY ACCESSORIES

Beyond the basics, consider enhancing your grilling repertoire with a few more accessories

- Cast Iron Cookware: Great for giving that perfect sear to meats or baking side dishes and desserts directly on the grill.
- Grill Baskets: Ideal for cooking smaller items like vegetables and shrimp that might fall through the grates.
- Pizza Stone: Transform your grill into a pizza oven and enjoy a smoky-flavored pizza crust.
- Digital Thermometer: For a quick and accurate reading of your grill's temperature, a digital thermometer can be extremely handy, especially when cooking delicate items.

Equipping yourself with these tools enriches your grilling experience and ensures that each meal you prepare on your Traeger is as delightful and successful as possible. Remember, each accessory is a step towards perfecting your grilling technique, maintaining your grill, and expanding the range of dishes you can confidently cook outdoors. With these tools by your side, you're well on your way to becoming a Traeger grill master, ready to impress with your grilling skills at the next family gathering or neighborhood barbecue.

GETTING STARTED: SETUP AND FIRST USE

Now that you're acquainted with your grill and have the right tools at hand, it's time to begin your grilling adventures. However, ensuring your Traeger grill is set up correctly is crucial to getting off to a great start. Here is a detailed guide to help you set up your grill effectively, which will serve as the foundation for all your future grilling endeavors.

CHOOSING THE PERFECT LOCATION

First things first, choosing the right location for your grill is critical. Your grill should be placed in a well-ventilated area to allow for proper airflow, which is essential for the grill to function safely and efficiently. Ensure it's set away from walls, overhangs, or any flammable materials to avoid potential fire hazards. Additionally, it's vital to position your grill on a stable, level surface. This ensures that it remains steady during use, preventing accidents and ensuring that your food cooks evenly.

ASSEMBLY

The next step is assembling your Traeger grill. It's important to follow the manufacturer's instructions closely to ensure every part is assembled correctly. All components should fit snugly and securely. Take your time with this process; double-check all connections and fittings to ensure everything is in place and correctly tightened. Proper assembly not only contributes to the safety of your grill but also affects its performance and longevity.

INITIAL FIRING

Before you begin to cook on your new grill, it's essential to "season" it. This process involves burning off any manufacturing residues that might still be present. Start by filling the hopper with your choice of wood pellets, then plug in the grill and turn it into the smoke setting. Let it run for about an hour. This initial firing will help you get accustomed to the basic operation of your Traeger and ensure that it is clean and ready to cook delicious meals.

UNDERSTANDING TEMPERATURE CONTROLS

Getting to know the temperature controls on your Traeger is crucial. Traeger grills are celebrated for their ability to maintain consistent temperatures, which is essential for both smoking at low temperatures and grilling at high temperatures. Spend some time experimenting with different settings to see how the grill reacts. This will help you understand how quickly it reaches the desired temperatures and how it maintains them during cooking. This knowledge will be invaluable when you start cooking different types of dishes, as each may require a specific temperature to achieve the best results.

SAFETY CHECKS

Safety should always be a priority when using any grill. Always check that the firepot is clean of old ash and that the grease management system is clear and functioning. These checks are vital to prevent flare-ups and ensure your grill operates efficiently. Making sure these components are clean and unobstructed not only enhances your safety but also the performance of your grill.

READY TO GRILL

With your Traeger grill set up and ready, you're well-prepared to dive into the delightful world of grilling. Whether it's your first time preparing a meal on a grill or if you're a seasoned pro, the simplicity and capabilities of the Traeger grill will transform how you think about cooking outdoors.

The versatility of your Traeger allows for endless culinary exploration, from smoking brisket to baking pizzas. Each session on your Traeger is an opportunity to perfect your grilling techniques and expand your recipe repertoire. Invite family and friends, try new

ecipes, and, most importantly, have fun. Grilling is about feeding the body and delighting
he senses and creating memories around the fire.

s you become more familiar with your grill, you'll find that starting it up and throwing
n just about anything from your kitchen becomes second nature. The smells, the sizzle,
nd the satisfaction of pulling a perfectly grilled steak or a beautifully smoked salmon off
he grate are pleasures that only a Traeger grill owner knows. So, take this foundation
ou've built today and let it guide you towards many joyful grilling seasons. Here's to great
rilling ahead!

CHAPTER 2: THE ART OF SMOKING

BASICS OF SMOKING

Welcome to the wonderful world of smoking with your Traeger grill, where you can transform simple ingredients into extraordinary meals with just a bit of smoke and time. Smoking is a cooking technique that uses low temperatures over long periods to slowly cook and infuse food with flavors from wood smoke. Unlike grilling, which often involves high heat and quick cooking times, smoking is all about patience and precision, allowing flavors to develop deeply.

To start smoking on your Traeger, it's essential to understand the setup process. Begin by ensuring your grill is clean and free of any previous cooking residues. This will help maintain the purity of the flavors you're about to create. Next, fill the pellet hopper with your chosen wood pellets, turn on the grill, and set it to the smoke setting. Allow the grill to preheat and come to a steady smoke temperature, typically around 225 to 250 degree Fahrenheit, which is the sweet spot for most smoking recipes.

The key to successful smoking is maintaining a consistent temperature throughout the cooking process. This is where your Traeger excels, thanks to its automated feed system that carefully manages the rate at which pellets are burned. Keeping the lid closed as much as possible avoids fluctuations in temperature that can affect cooking time and outcomes. Smoking with a Traeger grill is not just about setting and forgetting. It requires an understanding of how flavors develop over time and how different types of wood impact the taste of your food. Wood pellets come in a variety of flavors, and each type imparts a unique character to your dishes. For example, hickory pellets give a strong, savory smoke that is perfect for red meats, while apple pellets provide a sweeter, milder smoke that is ideal for poultry and fish.

The process begins with choosing the right wood pellets for the food you plan to smoke. Consider the final flavor profile you want to achieve and select a wood that complements your ingredients. Once you've loaded the pellets and set the temperature, it's time to prepare your meat, fish, or vegetables for smoking. This usually involves some seasoning, perhaps a rub or a marinade, which will meld with the smoke to create complex layers of flavor.

As your food smokes, it's crucial to monitor the internal temperature, especially for large cuts of meat. A meat probe thermometer is an invaluable tool here. It allows you to check the doneness without lifting the lid and letting heat escape, which can prolong the cooking process and alter the results. When smoking meats like brisket or pork shoulders, patience really is a virtue. These cuts can take several hours to reach the desired tenderness and flavor concentration, so plan your day accordingly.

During the smoking process, you might find it tempting to peek inside the grill often, but every time the lid is opened, smoke and heat escape, which can lead to uneven cooking and a loss of those precious smoky flavors. Instead, trust the process and let the Traeger do its job. You'll know it's worth the wait when you're greeted with the succulent smell of perfectly smoked food.

Another tip for enhancing the smoke flavor is to use a smoking tube or additional smoke boxes that can be placed in the grill to increase the amount of smoke generated. This is especially useful for shorter cooks who want a more pronounced smoke flavor without the extended cooking times.

After your food has reached its perfect internal temperature and absorbed enough smoke, it's important to let it rest. Resting allows the juices to redistribute throughout the meat, ensuring that each bite is juicy and flavorful. This is a good time to prepare any sides or sauces that will accompany your smoked masterpiece.

Smoking on a Traeger grill also offers the opportunity to experiment with combining different types of wood pellets to create unique flavor profiles. This blending of woods can tailor the smoke to match specific culinary creations, adding a personal touch to each dish. The versatility of flavors, from mesquite to cherry, opens up a world of possibilities for every meal, whether it's a casual weekend BBQ or a special holiday feast.

Each smoking session is a chance to refine your skills, experiment with new flavors, and enjoy the process of creating something truly delicious. So gather your ingredients, choose your pellets, and let the slow, rewarding process of smoking begin.

WOOD PELLETS: FLAVORS AND PAIRINGS

One of the most intriguing aspects of cooking with a Traeger grill is the ability to influence the flavor of your dishes through the choice of wood pellets. Each type of wood pellet offers a distinct flavor profile, acting much like a seasoning that enhances and complements the natural tastes of various foods. This gives you the freedom to tailor the smoky nuances of your dishes, elevating them beyond their basic elements.

HICKORY

Hickory is a powerhouse in the world of smoking woods, known for its strong, hearty BBQ flavor that is synonymous with traditional American barbecue.
This robust wood imparts a rich, pronounced smokiness that is ideal for meats like pork and ribs

The full-bodied flavor of hickory stands up exceptionally well to rich, fatty cuts, infusing them with a depth that is hard to achieve with lighter woods. When smoking with hickory expect your meats to develop a dark, tempting crust that is just as delightful to look at as it is to eat.

APPLE

In contrast to the boldness of hickory, apple wood pellets offer a gentler, slightly sweet smoke that works wonders on lighter meats. Apple wood's subtle sweetness complements poultry and pork without overwhelming the delicate flavors of the meat. It's particularly effective for dishes where you desire a hint of smoke without the intensity that stronger woods like mesquite or hickory might impart. Apple wood is excellent for a long, slow smoke, especially on foods that might dry out with more intense smoke flavors.

MESQUITE

Mesquite wood pellets are known for their bold, earthy flavor, imparting a touch of the rustic outdoors to every bite. This intense wood is a staple in Southwestern and Texan cuisines, renowned for its compatibility with beef and lamb. Mesquite burns hotter and faster than many other woods, producing a strong smoke that is perfect for grilling briskets, steaks, and other beef cuts that benefit from a hearty smoke flavor. However, due to its strength, mesquite should be used sparingly to avoid overpowering the dish.

CHERRY

Cherry wood is as versatile as it is delightful, offering a mild and fruity smoke that enhances the flavor of almost any type of meat. It's particularly effective on chicken and turkey, where it imparts a light, sweet smokiness that complements the natural flavors of the poultry. The subtle undertones of cherry are not limited to meats; they also work beautifully with cheeses and vegetables, adding a touch of sweetness that brightens the overall flavor profile of these dishes. Moreover, cherry wood can give your meats a rich mahogany color, making them visually appealing.

EXPERIMENTING WITH WOOD PELLETS

The real joy of smoking with a Traeger comes from experimenting with these different wood pellets to discover which flavors best complement your culinary creations. Each type of wood can dramatically alter the taste profile of your dish, much like spices in a recipe. For instance, blending apple and hickory pellets can achieve a balance of sweet and robust flavors, which is perfect for a pork shoulder that benefit rom both the depth of hickory and the light sweetness of apple.

ou might also experiment by mixing mesquite with cherry for a balance of bold and sweet, ideal for red
eats that can stand up to the intensity of mesquite while benefiting from the color and slight sweetness
f cherry. The combinations are as limitless as your imagination and palate desire.

s you explore these flavors, remember that the amount of smoke can also be adjusted. For a heavier
moke flavor, add more pellets and increase the cooking time at lower temperatures. For a subtler taste,
educe the pellets and smoke for a shorter period. This customization is what makes pellet grilling so
ersatile and exciting.

Vhether you're a seasoned smoker looking to refine your technique or a newcomer eager to explore the
ich flavors of wood-smoked food, understanding and utilizing different wood pellets can transform
our cooking. Each session with your Traeger grill offers an opportunity to perfect your smoking skills
nd impress with uniquely flavored dishes. So light up your grill, choose your pellets, and let the alchemy
f smoke and wood turn simple ingredients into culinary gold.

DVANCED SMOKING TECHNIQUES

s you become more comfortable with basic smoking, you may want to explore some advanced techniques
nat can elevate your smoking game. These methods require a bit more skill and attention but can lead
) even more impressive culinary results. Mastering these techniques can transform your approach to
moking, allowing you to create dishes that are infused with complexity and depth, tantalizing the taste
uds in new and exciting ways.

AYERING FLAVORS

sophisticated technique involves layering flavors by using different types of wood pellets at different
ages of cooking. For instance, you might start with a stronger wood-like hickory during the first few
ours of smoking to establish a robust flavor base. Then, as the cooking process nears its end, switch to
milder wood-like apple to infuse a gentle, sweet smokiness. This approach allows you to create a more
omplex flavor profile in your dishes, much like a chef uses spices to build layers of flavor in a dish. The
radual shift in smoke types brings an element of culinary artistry to your grilling, offering a nuanced
aste that can be adjusted to match the specific preferences of your palate.

USING A WATER PAN

Adding a water pan inside your grill can significantly impact the outcome of your smoked meats, especially when dealing with lean cuts that tend to dry out. The water pan acts as a humidity regulator within the grill, maintaining a moist environment that helps keep the meat juicy and tender throughout the cooking process. As the water in the pan heats up, it creates steam that mixes with the smoke, enveloping the meat in a moist, flavorful cloud. This not only prevents the meat from drying out but also helps enhance the smoke adherence to the surface, deepening the smoky flavor without overpowering the natural taste of the meat.

COLD SMOKING

Cold smoking is a technique used to infuse flavor without cooking the food, making it perfect for items like cheese, nuts, and certain types of fish, such as salmon. This method requires maintaining a much lower temperature, usually below 90 degrees Fahrenheit, which can be challenging but rewarding. To achieve this on a Traeger, you might consider using a pellet tube smoker, which can add smoke without significantly raising the grill's internal temperature. Cold smoking allows the smoke to penetrate deeply into the food, imparting a rich, smoky flavor that enhances the food's natural characteristics without cooking it, preserving the original textures and adding a gourmet touch.

REVERSE SEARING

Reverse searing is an excellent technique for achieving the perfect finish on thick steaks or chops. This method involves initially smoking the meat at a low temperature to infuse it with your desired level of smoky flavor, then cranking up the heat at the end of the cooking process to sear the exterior. The result is meat that is cooked evenly throughout with a tender, juicy interior and a crisp, caramelized crust. This technique enhances the flavor and improves the texture, giving you a steakhouse-quality finish that can make even a simple meal feel luxurious.

REFINING YOUR TECHNIQUE

Mastering these advanced techniques can take your grilling to the next level, providing you with a toolkit to impress even the most discerning palates. As you experiment with these methods, you'll gain a deeper understanding of how different factors, such as type of wood, temperature, and timing, influence the final outcome of your cooking. Each session at your Traeger grill offers a learning opportunity—a chance to refine your skill nd expand your culinary repertoire.

Remember, the key to successful smoking is patience and attention to detail. Whether you're layering flavors, utilizing a water pan, experimenting with cold smoking, or perfecting the reverse sear, each technique offers a path to enhance your culinary creations. Embrace the slower pace of smoking as a chance to savor the cooking process just as much as the eating process.

Smoking with your Traeger grill opens up a world of culinary possibilities. Whether you're a beginner looking to master the basics or an experienced pitmaster eager to experiment with advanced techniques, the art of smoking can provide some of the most flavorful and satisfying meals. So, take your time, enjoy the process, and let the magic of smoke work its wonders on your ingredients. With each dish, you'll feed your guests and delight their senses, making every meal an occasion to remember.

CHAPTER 3: GRILLING BASICS

Grilling is an art that beautifully combines intuition with technique, turning simple raw ingredients into delectable culinary creations. This chapter is dedicated to exploring the essential grilling basics every Traeger grill owner should master—from achieving perfect temperature control and understanding flame management, to ensuring proper maintenance of your grill. These fundamentals lay the foundation for countless successful cookouts and unforgettable meals.

TEMPERATURE CONTROL AND TIMING

Effective temperature control is the cornerstone of successful grilling. While the Traeger grill simplifies this with its digital controls and consistent heat supply, learning how to effectively leverage these features is crucial for any griller.

UNDERSTANDING THE HEAT

The temperature required for grilling can vary significantly depending on the type of food you're preparing. Thick cuts of meat like brisket, for example, require a lower temperature over a longer period to tenderize properly and achieve that coveted fall-off-the-bone texture. In contrast, vegetables and thinner cuts of meat like burgers and steaks benefit from a hotter, quicker cook. This method seals in the juices and creates a satisfyingly crispy outer crust.

Start by familiarizing yourself with the temperature settings on your Traeger. Most models offer a versatile range of temperatures, typically from as low as 165°F to as high as 500°F. Knowing which temperatures work best for different types of food will enhance your grilling efficiency and success. For example, smoking a pork shoulder may best be done at around 225°F, whereas searing a steak might require the heat cranked up to 450° or higher.

TIMING IS EVERYTHING

The secret to perfect grilling lies not only in setting the right temperature but also in mastering the timing. Despite the consistent heat provided by a Traeger, knowing how long to cook various items is crucial. A meat thermometer becomes an invaluable tool in this context. It's not merely about cooking meat to safe temperatures; it's about achieving the perfect degree of doneness. For instance, poultry should reach an internal temperature of 165°F to ensure it is safe to eat, while steaks can vary from 125°F for a rare finish to 160°F for well-done. Using a thermometer helps take the guesswork out of grilling, leading to consistently successful outcomes. For precise grilling, familiarize yourself with the recommended cooking times and temperatures for various foods. This will improve your grilling results and enhance your confidence as you grill.

MANAGING THE HEAT

Managing the temperature during grilling involves more than setting your grill and walking away. It requires attention to how foods react to heat. Fat drippings, flare-ups, and even ambient temperatures can affect the internal grill temperature. Learn to adjust the settings dynamically as you cook. If you notice the temperature fluctuating more than usual, check for potential causes, such as pellet levels in the hopper or whether the lid has been opened too frequently. Keeping a steady temperature is critical to evenly cooked food.

MANAGING THE FLAME: TIPS AND TRICKS

Flame management on a Traeger differs from traditional grills since you are dealing with wood pellets and an electric system rather than direct flames. However, understanding how to control and manipulate this can significantly enhance your grilling.

ADJUSTING FOR WIND AND WEATHER

Outdoor cooking is often at the mercy of the elements, with wind and cold weather impacting how your grill retains heat. On windy days, it may be necessary to adjust the temperature higher to compensate for the increased air circulation, which can cool the grill faster than usual. Conversely, on very hot days, you might find that your grill heats up more quickly or goes beyond the set temperature, requiring adjustments to lower setting.

CREATING HEAT ZONES

Although a Traeger grill provides a uniform heating environment due to its design, creating different heat zones can be beneficial for cooking meals that require different temperatures simultaneously. You can manipulate this by placing foods that require lower temperatures further from the center, where the heat is often most intense, and vice versa. This method, usually referred to as indirect grilling, is perfect for items that need gentle cooking or for keeping food warm.

CHAPTER 4: BEEF ON THE GRILL

CLASSIC SMOKED BRISKET

TRADITIONAL TEXAS SMOKED BRISKET

8 SERVINGS   30 MINUTES   8 HOURS

INSTRUCTIONS:

1. *Preheat your smoker to 250°F (121°C).*
2. *Mix salt, pepper, and garlic powder together in a bowl.*
3. *Rub the spice mix all over the brisket evenly.*
4. *Place the brisket in the smoker, fat side up, and close the lid.*
5. *Smoke for about 8 hours, or until the internal temperature reaches 195°F (91°C).*
6. *Remove from smoker and let rest for 30 minutes before slicing against the grain.*

INGREDIENTS:

- 1 whole brisket, trimmed (12 lbs or 5 kg)
- 1/4 cup salt (60 g)
- 1/4 cup black pepper (60 g)
- 2 tbsp garlic powder (30 g)

NUTRITIONAL FACTS:

400 Kcal, 0g Cho, 30g Fat, 880mg Na, 30g Pro

SWEET AND SPICY BRISKET

 8 SERVINGS

 20 MINUTES

 8 HOURS

NUTRITIONAL FACTS:

420 Kcal, 5g Cho, 32g Fat, 900mg Na, 31g Pro

INSTRUCTIONS:

1. Preheat your smoker to 250°F (121°C).
2. Combine brown sugar, chili powder, paprika, cayenne pepper, salt, and black pepper in a bowl.
3. Apply the rub generously over the entire surface of the brisket.
4. Place brisket in the smoker, fat side up.
5. Smoke for about 8 hours, or until it reaches an internal temperature of 195°F (91°C).
6. Allow brisket to rest for 20 minutes before slicing.

INGREDIENTS:

- 1 whole brisket, trimmed (10 lbs or 4.5 kg)
- 2 tbsp brown sugar (30 g)
- 1 tbsp chili powder (15 g)
- 1 tbsp paprika (15 g)
- 2 tsp cayenne pepper (10 g)
- 2 tbsp salt (30 g)
- 1 tbsp black pepper (15 g)

COFFEE-CRUSTED BRISKET

8 SERVINGS   15 MINUTES   8 HOURS

INGREDIENTS:

- 1 whole brisket, trimmed (10 lbs or 4.5 kg)
- 1/4 cup ground coffee (60 g)
- 1/4 cup brown sugar (60 g)
- 2 tbsp salt (30 g)
- 1 tbsp black pepper (15 g)
- 1 tbsp garlic powder (15 g)

INSTRUCTIONS:

1. *Preheat the smoker to 250°F (121°C).*
2. *Combine ground coffee, brown sugar, salt, pepper, and garlic powder in a bowl.*
3. *Rub the mixture all over the brisket evenly.*
4. *Place brisket in the smoker, fat side up.*
5. *Smoke for about 8 hours, until the internal temperature is 195°F (91°C).*
6. *Let the brisket rest for about 30 minutes before slicing.*

NUTRITIONAL FACTS:

410 Kcal, 6g Cho, 32g Fat, 890mg Na, 30g Pro

BRISKET WITH MAPLE-BOURBON GLAZE

 8 SERVINGS

 20 MINUTES

 8 HOURS

 NUTRITIONAL FACTS:

480 Kcal, 15g Cho, 32g Fat, 880mg Na, 31g Pro

INGREDIENTS:

- 1 whole brisket, trimmed (11 lbs or 5 kg)
- 1/4 cup bourbon (60 ml)
- 1/4 cup maple syrup (60 ml)
- 1/4 cup brown sugar (60 g)
- 1/4 cup Worcestershire sauce (60 ml)
- 2 tbsp salt (30 g)
- 1 tbsp black pepper (15 g)

INSTRUCTIONS:

1. Preheat your smoker to 250°F (121°C).
2. Mix bourbon, maple syrup, brown sugar, and Worcestershire sauce in a bowl.
3. Season the brisket with salt and black pepper.
4. Place brisket in smoker, fat side up, and apply half of the glaze.
5. Halfway through smoking, apply the remaining glaze.
6. Continue to smoke until the internal temperature reaches 195°F (91°C).
7. Rest the brisket for 30 minutes before slicing.

BRISKET WITH APPLE CIDER VINEGAR MOP

8 SERVINGS   10 MINUTES   8 HOURS

INGREDIENTS:

- 1 whole brisket, trimmed (10 lbs or 4.5 kg)
- 1 cup apple cider vinegar (240 ml)
- 1/2 cup water (120 ml)
- 1/4 cup olive oil (60 ml)
- 3 tbsp salt (45 g)
- 1 tbsp black pepper (15 g)
- 2 tbsp paprika (30 g)

INSTRUCTIONS:

1. *Preheat the smoker to 250°F (121°C).*
2. *Mix apple cider vinegar, water, and olive oil in a bowl.*
3. *Combine salt, pepper, and paprika, and rub it on the brisket.*
4. *Place the brisket in the smoker, fat side up.*
5. *Mop the brisket with the vinegar mixture every hour during cooking.*
6. *Continue smoking until the brisket reaches an internal temperature of 195°F (91°C).*
7. *Allow the brisket to rest for about 30 minutes before slicing.*

NUTRITIONAL FACTS:

390 Kcal, 0g Cho, 30g Fat, 950mg Na, 28g Pro

PERFECT GRILLED STEAKS

CLASSIC RIBEYE WITH HERB BUTTER

8 SERVINGS   15 MINUTES   10 MINUTES

INGREDIENTS:

- 4 ribeye steaks (8 oz each or 227 g each)
- 2 tsp salt (10 g)
- 2 tsp black pepper (10 g)
- 1/2 cup unsalted butter, softened (113 g)
- 1 tbsp chopped fresh parsley (15 g)
- 1 tbsp chopped fresh chives (15 g)
- 1 tsp chopped fresh thyme (5 g)

INSTRUCTIONS:

1. *Preheat grill to high, around 500°F (260°C).*
2. *Season steaks with salt and pepper.*
3. *Grill steaks for 5 minutes on each side for medium-rare.*
4. *Mix butter with parsley, chives, and thyme.*
5. *Top each steak with a dollop of herb butter before serving.*

NUTRITIONAL FACTS:

450 Kcal, 1g Cho, 35g Fat, 590mg Na, 34g Pro

GARLIC-THYME FILET MIGNON

 8 SERVINGS

 10 MINUTES

 12 MINUTES

NUTRITIONAL FACTS:

420 Kcal, 5g Cho, 32g Fat, 900mg Na, 31g Pro

INSTRUCTIONS:

1. Preheat grill to medium-high, about 450°F (232°C).
2. Rub each steak with olive oil, garlic, thyme, salt, and pepper.
3. Grill steaks for 6 minutes per side or until desired doneness.
4. Let steaks rest for 5 minutes before serving.
5. Nutritional Information: 320 Kcal, 1g Cho, 20g Fat, 610mg Na, 34g Pro

INGREDIENTS:

- 4 filet mignon steaks (8 oz each or 227 g each)
- 2 tsp salt (10 g)
- 2 tsp black pepper (10 g)
- 2 tbsp olive oil (30 ml)
- 4 cloves garlic, minced (12 g)
- 2 tsp fresh thyme, minced (10 g)

SPICY CHIMICHURRI SIRLOIN STEAK

8 SERVINGS   20 MINUTES   10 MINUTES

INSTRUCTIONS:

1. *Combine parsley, olive oil, vinegar, garlic, red pepper flakes, salt, and pepper to make the chimichurri.*
2. *Marinate steaks in half of the chimichurri for 15 minutes.*
3. *Preheat grill to high, around 500°F (260°C).*
4. *Grill steaks for 5 minutes on each side.*
5. *Serve steaks with the remaining chimichurri on top.*

INGREDIENTS:

- 4 sirloin steaks (8 oz each or 227 g each)
- 2 tsp salt (10 g)
- 2 tsp black pepper (10 g)
- 1/2 cup fresh parsley, chopped (30 g)
- 1/4 cup olive oil (60 ml)
- 3 tbsp red wine vinegar (45 ml)
- 2 cloves garlic, minced (6 g)
- 1 tsp red pepper flakes (5 g)

NUTRITIONAL FACTS:

330 Kcal, 2g Cho, 25g Fat, 620mg Na, 34g Pro

BOURBON-MARINATED FLANK STEAK

 8 SERVINGS

NUTRITIONAL FACTS:

390 Kcal, 9g Cho, 14g Fat, 870mg Na, 35g Pro

 140 MINUTES

 10 MINUTES

INSTRUCTIONS:

1. Whisk together bourbon, soy sauce, brown sugar, garlic, and pepper.
2. Marinate the steak in the mixture for at least 2 hours in the refrigerator.
3. Preheat grill to high, around 500°F (260°C).
4. Grill steak for 5 minutes on each side.
5. Let steak rest for 10 minutes, then slice against the grain.

INGREDIENTS:

- 2 lbs flank steak (907 g)
- 1/2 cup bourbon (120 ml)
- 1/4 cup soy sauce (60 ml)
- 1/4 cup brown sugar (55 g)
- 3 cloves garlic, minced (9 g)
- 1 tsp black pepper (5 g)

BLACK PEPPER AND ROSEMARY T-BONE STEAK

8 SERVINGS   10 MINUTES   14 MINUTES

INGREDIENTS:

- 4 T-bone steaks (1 lb each or 453 g each)
- 2 tbsp coarse black pepper (30 g)
- 2 tbsp fresh rosemary, minced (30 g)
- 2 tsp salt (10 g)
- 2 tbsp olive oil (30 ml)

INSTRUCTIONS:

1. *Rub each steak with olive oil, then season with black pepper, rosemary, and salt.*
2. *reheat grill to medium-high, about 450°F (232°C).*
3. *Grill steaks for 7 minutes on each side or until desired doneness.*
4. *Let steaks rest for 5 minutes before serving.*

NUTRITIONAL FACTS:

410 Kcal, 0g Cho, 28g Fat, 590mg Na, 38g Pro

UNIQUE BEEF DISHES

KOREAN BULGOGI BBQ BEEF

8 SERVINGS   140 MINUTES   10 MINUTES

INGREDIENTS:

- 2 lbs thinly sliced beef sirloin (907 g)
- 1/2 cup soy sauce (120 ml)
- 2 tbsp sesame oil (30 ml)
- 1/4 cup brown sugar (55 g)
- 4 cloves garlic, minced (16 g)
- 2 tbsp freshly grated ginger (30 g)
- 2 tbsp sesame seeds (30 g)
- 4 green onions, chopped (50 g)

INSTRUCTIONS:

1. *Combine soy sauce, sesame oil, brown sugar, garlic, and ginger in a bowl to create the marinade.*
2. *Add beef to the marinade and refrigerate for at least 2 hours.*
3. *Preheat the grill to medium-high, about 450°F (232°C).*
4. *Grill beef slices for 2 to 3 minutes on each side.*
5. *Garnish with sesame seeds and green onions before serving.*

NUTRITIONAL FACTS:

310 Kcal, 14g Cho, 20g Fat, 850mg Na, 23g Pro

BEEF WELLINGTON WITH SMOKED MUSHROOM DUXELLES

 8 SERVINGS

 45 MINUTES

 45 MINUTES

NUTRITIONAL FACTS:

510 Kcal, 32g Cho, 28g Fat, 460mg Na, 34g Pro

INSTRUCTIONS:

1. Sear beef in olive oil over high heat until browned on all sides.
2. Sauté mushrooms and shallots until moisture evaporates, then deglaze with wine.
3. Spread mushroom mixture (duxelles) over cooled beef.
4. Wrap beef and duxelles in puff pastry and brush with egg.
5. Bake at 400°F (204°C) for 45 minutes or until pastry is golden.

INGREDIENTS:

- 2 lbs beef tenderloin (907 g)
- 2 tbsp olive oil (30 ml)
- 1 lb mushrooms, finely chopped (453 g)
- 2 shallots, minced (60 g)
- 1/4 cup dry white wine (60 ml)
- 2 tsp thyme, minced (10 g)
- 1 package puff pastry, thawed (450 g)
- 1 egg, beaten (50 g)

ARGENTINE GRILLED TRI-TIP WITH CHIMICHURRI

 8 SERVINGS

 15 MINUTES

 40 MINUTES

INSTRUCTIONS:

1. *Combine olive oil, vinegar, parsley, garlic, red pepper flakes, salt, and pepper to make chimichurri.*
2. *Reserve half of the chimichurri for serving.*
3. *Marinate tri-tip in the remaining chimichurri for at least 30 minutes.*
4. *Grill over medium heat, about 350°F (177°C), for 20 minutes per side.*
5. *Slice and serve with reserved chimichurri.*

INGREDIENTS:

- 2 lbs tri-tip steak (907 g)
- 1/2 cup olive oil (120 ml)
- 1/3 cup red wine vinegar (80 ml)
- 1/2 cup chopped parsley (30 g)
- 4 cloves garlic, minced (16 g)
- 1 tsp red pepper flakes (5 g)
- 1 tsp salt (5 g)
- 1 tsp black pepper (5 g)

NUTRITIONAL FACTS:

380 Kcal, 2g Cho, 30g Fat, 600mg Na, 24g Pro

SMOKED BEEF TACOS WITH AVOCADO SALSA

 8 SERVINGS

 30 MINUTES

 120 MINUTES

NUTRITIONAL FACTS:

350 Kcal, 20g Cho, 22g Fat, 480mg Na, 24g Pro

INSTRUCTIONS:

1. Rub brisket with paprika, cumin, salt, and pepper.
2. Smoke over low heat, about 225°F (107°C), until tender, about 2 hours.
3. Combine avocados, onion, cilantro, and lime juice to make salsa.
4. Shred the brisket and serve in tortillas topped with avocado salsa.

INGREDIENTS:

- 2 lbs beef brisket (907 g)
- 2 tbsp smoked paprika (30 g)
- 1 tbsp cumin (15 g)
- 2 tsp salt (10 g)
- 1 tsp black pepper (5 g)
- 2 avocados, diced (300 g)
- 1/2 red onion, finely chopped (60 g)
- 1/4 cup chopped cilantro (15 g)
- Juice of 2 limes (60 ml)
- 16 small corn tortillas (320 g)

MEDITERRANEAN STUFFED BEEF ROLLS

8 SERVINGS   20 MINUTES   20 MINUTES

INGREDIENTS:

- 2 lbs flank steak, thinly sliced (907 g)
- 1/2 cup crumbled feta cheese (75 g)
- 1/2 cup spinach, chopped (30 g)
- 1/4 cup sun-dried tomatoes, chopped (37 g)
- 2 tbsp balsamic vinegar (30 ml)
- 1 tbsp olive oil (15 ml)
- 1 tsp salt (5 g)
- 1 tsp black pepper (5 g)

INSTRUCTIONS:

1. *Lay out beef slices and season with salt and pepper.*
2. *Top each slice with feta, spinach, and sun-dried tomatoes.*
3. *Roll up the beef slices tightly and secure them with toothpicks.*
4. *Heat olive oil in a pan and sear rolls on all sides.*
5. *Drizzle with balsamic vinegar and cook covered over low heat for 15 minutes*

NUTRITIONAL FACTS:

310 Kcal, 4g Cho, 18g Fat, 620mg Na, 30g Pro

SMOKED MEATLOAF WITH BBQ GLAZE

 8 SERVINGS

NUTRITIONAL FACTS:

560 Kcal, 42g Cho, 24g Fat, 880mg Na, 36g Pro

 20 MINUTES

 120 MINUTES

INGREDIENTS:

- 2 lbs ground beef (907 g)
- 1 cup breadcrumbs (120 g)
- 1/2 cup milk (120 ml)
- 2 eggs (100 g)
- 1 onion, finely chopped (150 g)
- 2 cloves garlic, minced (8 g)
- 1 tbsp salt (15 g)
- 1 tsp black pepper (5 g)
- 1 cup BBQ sauce (240 ml)

INSTRUCTIONS:

1. Preheat smoker to 250°F (121°C).
2. In a large bowl, combine ground beef, breadcrumbs, milk, eggs, onion, garlic, salt, and pepper.
3. Shape the mixture into a loaf and place it on a wire rack in the smoker.
4. Smoke for about 1 hour 30 minutes.
5. Glaze the meatloaf with BBQ sauce and continue smoking for another 30 minutes.
6. Remove from smoker and let rest for 10 minutes before slicing.

CARIBBEAN JERK BEEF SKEWERS

8 SERVINGS   135 MINUTES   15 MINUTES

INGREDIENTS:

- 2 lbs beef sirloin, cut into cubes (907 g)
- 3 tbsp jerk seasoning (45 g)
- 2 tbsp soy sauce (30 ml)
- 1 tbsp honey (15 ml)
- Juice of 1 lime (30 ml)
- 2 bell peppers, cut into pieces (300 g)
- 1 large onion, cut into chunks (150 g)

INSTRUCTIONS:

1. *Combine jerk seasoning, soy sauce, honey, and lime juice in a bowl.*
2. *Add beef cubes to the marinade and refrigerate for 2 hours.*
3. *Preheat grill to medium-high, about 450°F (232°C).*
4. *Thread beef, bell peppers, and onions onto skewers.*
5. *Grill for about 15 minutes, turning occasionally, until beef is cooked to the desired doneness.*

NUTRITIONAL FACTS:

300 Kcal, 16g Cho, 10g Fat, 700mg Na, 36g Pro

ITALIAN BEEF BRACIOLE

 8 SERVINGS

 30 MINUTES

 120 MINUTES

NUTRITIONAL FACTS:

350 Kcal, 20g Cho, 22g Fat, 480mg Na, 24g Pro

INGREDIENTS:

- 2 lbs flank steak (907 g)
- 4 cloves garlic, minced (16 g)
- 1/2 cup grated Parmesan cheese (50 g)
- 1/4 cup chopped parsley (15 g)
- 1/4 cup breadcrumbs (30 g)
- 2 cups marinara sauce (480 ml)
- 2 tbsp olive oil (30 ml)
- 1 tsp salt (5 g)
- 1 tsp black pepper (5 g)

INSTRUCTIONS:

1. Flatten flank steak to about 1/4 inch thickness.
2. Spread garlic, Parmesan, parsley, and breadcrumbs over steak.
3. Roll up steak tightly and secure it with kitchen twine.
4. Heat olive oil in a pan and brown the braciole on all sides.
5. Transfer to a baking dish, pour marinara sauce over the top, and cover.
6. Bake at 350°F (177°C) for about 1 hour 30 minutes.

MOROCCAN SPICED BEEF TAGINE

8 SERVINGS   20 MINUTES   120 MINUTES

INGREDIENTS:

- 2 lbs beef chuck, cut into cubes (907 g)
- 2 tbsp Moroccan spice blend (30 g)
- 1 can diced tomatoes (400 g)
- 1 onion, chopped (150 g)
- 3 carrots, sliced (150 g)
- 1 cup beef broth (240 ml)
- 1/4 cup chopped dried apricots (30 g)
- 2 tbsp olive oil (30 ml)
- 1 tsp salt (5 g)
- 1 tsp black pepper (5 g)

INSTRUCTIONS:

1. *Heat olive oil in a tagine or large pot.*
2. *Brown the beef cubes with Moroccan spices.*
3. *Add onions and carrots, cooking until softened.*
4. *Stir in tomatoes, beef broth, and apricots.*
5. *Cover and simmer on low heat for about 1 hour 45 minutes.*

NUTRITIONAL FACTS:

350 Kcal, 15g Cho, 18g Fat, 600mg Na, 36g Pro

SMOKED BEEF BOLOGNESE

 8 SERVINGS

 20 MINUTES

 240 MINUTES

NUTRITIONAL FACTS:

460 Kcal, 12g Cho, 30g Fat, 620mg Na, 36g Pro

INGREDIENTS:

- 2 lbs ground beef (907 g)
- 1 can crushed tomatoes (28 oz or 794 g)
- 1 onion, finely chopped (150 g)
- 2 carrots, finely chopped (100 g)
- 4 cloves garlic, minced (16 g)
- 1/4 cup red wine (60 ml)
- 2 tbsp olive oil (30 ml)
- 1 tbsp Italian seasoning (15 g)
- 1 tsp salt (5 g)
- 1 tsp black pepper (5 g)

INSTRUCTIONS:

1. Heat olive oil in a large pot over medium heat.
2. Add ground beef, onion, carrots, and garlic, and cook until the meat is browned.
3. Pour in red wine and let simmer until reduced.
4. Add crushed tomatoes and Italian seasoning.
5. Transfer mixture to a smoker set at 225°F (107°C) and smoke for 3 hours.
6. Serve over cooked pasta or polenta.

STOUT-INFUSED BEEF AND ONION PIE

 8 SERVINGS

 30 MINUTES

 150 MINUTES

INSTRUCTIONS:

1. *Preheat oven to 375°F (190°C).*
2. *Brown beef in a large pot over medium-high heat.*
3. *Add onions and cook until softened.*
4. *Stir in flour, then gradually add stout and beef broth.*
5. *Simmer for 1 hour until beef is tender.*
6. *Pour beef mixture into a pie dish and cover with puff pastry.*
7. *Brush pastry with beaten egg.*
8. *Bake for 30 minutes or until golden brown.*

INGREDIENTS:

- 2 lbs beef chuck, cubed (907 g)
- 1 large onion, sliced (150 g)
- 2 cups stout beer (480 ml)
- 2 cups beef broth (480 ml)
- 1/4 cup all-purpose flour (30 g)
- 1 tsp salt (5 g)
- 1 tsp black pepper (5 g)
- 1 package puff pastry, thawed (450 g)
- 1 egg, beaten (50 g)

NUTRITIONAL FACTS:

520 Kcal, 38g Cho, 30g Fat, 690mg Na, 28g Pro

SMOKED BEEF RIBS WITH HONEY-GARLIC SAUCE

 8 SERVINGS

 15 MINUTES

 240 MINUTES

NUTRITIONAL FACTS:

610 Kcal, 45g Cho, 35g Fat, 800mg Na, 25g Pro

INSTRUCTIONS:

1. Preheat smoker to 225°F (107°C).
2. Combine honey, soy sauce, garlic, ginger, and black pepper in a bowl.
3. Brush ribs with half the sauce.
4. Smoke ribs for 4 hours, basting occasionally with remaining sauce.
5. Serve ribs with any leftover sauce.

INGREDIENTS:

- 4 lbs beef ribs (1814 g)
- 1 cup honey (240 ml)
- 1/2 cup soy sauce (120 ml)
- 4 cloves garlic, minced (16 g)
- 1 tbsp ginger, minced (15 g)
- 1 tsp black pepper (5 g)

GRILLED BEEF GYROS WITH TZATZIKI

8 SERVINGS   20 MINUTES   10 MINUTES

INSTRUCTIONS:

1. *Marinate beef with oregano, garlic, olive oil, lemon juice, salt, and pepper for 15 minutes.*
2. *Grill beef over medium-high heat for 10 minutes, turning once.*
3. *Mix cucumber, Greek yogurt, and dill to make tzatziki.*
4. *Serve grilled beef in pita pieces of bread topped with tzatziki.*

INGREDIENTS:

- 2 lbs thinly sliced sirloin steak (907 g)
- 2 tsp oregano (10 g)
- 4 cloves garlic, minced (16 g)
- 2 tbsp olive oil (30 ml)
- Juice of 1 lemon (30 ml)
- Salt and pepper to taste
- 1 cucumber, grated (150 g)
- 2 cups Greek yogurt (480 ml)
- 1/4 cup fresh dill, chopped (15 g)
- 8 pita breads (640 g)

NUTRITIONAL FACTS:

480 Kcal, 40g Cho, 20g Fat, 590mg Na, 34g Pro

SZECHUAN BEEF WITH BROCCOLI

 8 SERVINGS

 15 MINUTES

 20 MINUTES

NUTRITIONAL FACTS:

350 Kcal, 15g Cho, 18g Fat, 630mg Na, 36g Pro

INSTRUCTIONS:

1. Heat oil in a large skillet over high heat.
2. Add beef and stir-fry until browned.
3. Add broccoli and cook for 5 minutes.
4. Mix soy sauce, hoisin sauce, chili paste, garlic, ginger, cornstarch, and water.
5. Pour sauce over beef and broccoli and cook until thickened

INGREDIENTS:

- 2 lbs flank steak, thinly sliced (907 g)
- 4 cups broccoli florets (360 g)
- 2 tbsp vegetable oil (30 ml)
- 1/4 cup soy sauce (60 ml)
- 2 tbsp hoisin sauce (30 ml)
- 1 tbsp chili paste (15 g)
- 2 cloves garlic, minced (8 g)
- 1 tbsp ginger, minced (15 g)
- 1 tsp cornstarch (5 g)
- 1/4 cup water (60 ml)

MEXICAN BEEF BARBACOA

8 SERVINGS   30 MINUTES   240 MINUTES

INSTRUCTIONS:

1. *Place beef chunks in a slow cooker.*
2. *Combine chipotle chilis, garlic, onion, vinegar, cumin, oregano, salt, pepper, and beef broth.*
3. *Pour mixture over beef in the slow cooker.*
4. *Cook on low for 8 hours until meat is tender and shreds easily.*
5. *Shred beef and serve with tortillas or rice.*

INGREDIENTS:

- 3 lbs chuck roast, cut into chunks (1360 g)
- 3 chipotle chilis in adobo sauce, minced (45 g)
- 4 cloves garlic, minced (16 g)
- 1 onion, chopped (150 g)
- 1/4 cup apple cider vinegar (60 ml)
- 1 tbsp cumin (15 g)
- 1 tbsp dried oregano (15 g)
- 1 tsp salt (5 g)
- 1 tsp black pepper (5 g)
- 2 cups beef broth (480 ml)

NUTRITIONAL FACTS:

360 Kcal, 5g Cho, 24g Fat, 690mg Na, 34g Pro

SMOKED BEEF RIBS WITH HONEY-GARLIC SAUCE

 8 SERVINGS

 15 MINUTES

 240 MINUTES

NUTRITIONAL FACTS:

610 Kcal, 45g Cho, 35g Fat, 800mg Na, 25g Pro

INSTRUCTIONS:

1. Preheat smoker to 225°F (107°C).
2. Combine honey, soy sauce, garlic, ginger, and black pepper in a bowl.
3. Brush ribs with half the sauce.
4. Smoke ribs for 4 hours, basting occasionally with remaining sauce.
5. Serve ribs with any leftover sauce.

INGREDIENTS:

- 4 lbs beef ribs (1814 g)
- 1 cup honey (240 ml)
- 1/2 cup soy sauce (120 ml)
- 4 cloves garlic, minced (16 g)
- 1 tbsp ginger, minced (15 g)
- 1 tsp black pepper (5 g)

CHAPTER 5: PORK PERFECTION
PULLED PORK ESSENTIALS

CLASSIC SMOKED PULLED PORK

8 SERVINGS   20 MINUTES   480 MINUTES

INSTRUCTIONS:

1. *Mix salt, black pepper, paprika, and garlic powder together in a bowl.*
2. *Rub the spice mixture all over the pork shoulder.*
3. *Preheat your smoker to 225°F (107°C).*
4. *Place the pork shoulder in the smoker and cook for about 8 hours, or until it reaches an internal temperature of 195°F (91°C).*
5. *Remove from smoker and let rest for 30 minutes before pulling the meat apart with forks.*

INGREDIENTS:

- 5 lbs pork shoulder (2268 g)
- 2 tbsp salt (30 g)
- 2 tbsp black pepper (30 g)
- 2 tbsp paprika (30 g)
- 1 tbsp garlic powder (15 g)

NUTRITIONAL FACTS:

510 Kcal, 0g Cho, 35g Fat, 1500mg Na, 48g Pro

SWEET CAROLINA PULLED PORK

 8 SERVINGS

 15 MINUTES

480 MINUTES

NUTRITIONAL FACTS:

530 Kcal, 10g Cho, 35g Fat, 1550mg Na, 48g Pro

INSTRUCTIONS:

1. Combine brown sugar, vinegar, mustard powder, chili powder, garlic powder, and salt in a bowl.
2. Rub the mixture all over the pork shoulder.
3. Set your smoker to 225°F (107°C).
4. Smoke the pork shoulder for about 8 hours, or until it is tender and pulls apart easily.
5. Rest the pork for 30 minutes, then shred with forks and serve.

INGREDIENTS:

- 5 lbs pork shoulder (2268 g)
- 1/4 cup brown sugar (55 g)
- 2 tbsp apple cider vinegar (30 ml)
- 1 tbsp mustard powder (15 g)
- 1 tbsp chili powder (15 g)
- 1 tbsp garlic powder (15 g)
- 2 tsp salt (10 g)

SPICY CHIPOTLE PULLED PORK

8 SERVINGS   15 MINUTES   480 MINUTES

INSTRUCTIONS:

1. *Combine chipotle peppers, honey, garlic powder, onion powder, and salt in a bowl.*
2. *Rub the mixture thoroughly over the pork shoulder.*
3. *Preheat your smoker to 225°F (107°C).*
4. *Place the pork in the smoker and cook for about 8 hours until it reaches an internal temperature of 195°F (91°C).*
5. *Let the pork rest for 30 minutes before shredding with forks.*

INGREDIENTS:

- 5 lbs pork shoulder (2268 g)
- 1/4 cup chipotle peppers in adobo sauce, minced (60 ml)
- 3 tbsp honey (45 ml)
- 2 tbsp garlic powder (30 g)
- 2 tbsp onion powder (30 g)
- 1 tbsp salt (15 g)

NUTRITIONAL FACTS:

520 Kcal, 15g Cho, 35g Fat, 1580mg Na, 48g Pro

HAWAIIAN PULLED PORK WITH PINEAPPLE

 8 SERVINGS

  20 MINUTES

 480 MINUTES

NUTRITIONAL FACTS:

560 Kcal, 20g Cho, 35g Fat, 1600mg Na, 48g Pro

INSTRUCTIONS:

1. Mix pineapple, soy sauce, brown sugar, garlic powder, ginger, and salt in a bowl.
2. Rub the mixture all over the pork shoulder.
3. Preheat your smoker to 225°F (107°C).
4. Smoke the pork for 8 hours or until it reaches an internal temperature of 195°F (91°C).
5. Allow to rest for 30 minutes, then pull the pork using forks.

INGREDIENTS:

- 5 lbs pork shoulder (2268 g)
- 1 cup pineapple, diced (165 g)
- 1/4 cup soy sauce (60 ml)
- 1/4 cup brown sugar (55 g)
- 1 tbsp garlic powder (15 g)
- 1 tbsp ginger, minced (15 g)
- 2 tsp salt (10 g)

PULLED PORK WITH BOURBON BBQ SAUCE

8 SERVINGS

15 MINUTES

480 MINUTES

INGREDIENTS:

- 5 lbs pork shoulder (2268 g)
- 1 cup BBQ sauce (240 ml)
- 1/4 cup bourbon (60 ml)
- 2 tbsp brown sugar (30 g)
- 1 tbsp smoked paprika (15 g)
- 1 tbsp garlic powder (15 g)
- 2 tsp salt (10 g)

INSTRUCTIONS:

1. Combine BBQ sauce, bourbon, brown sugar, smoked paprika, garlic powder, and salt in a bowl.
2. Rub the sauce mixture over the pork shoulder.
3. Set your smoker to 225°F (107°C).
4. Smoke the pork for 8 hours, or until the internal temperature reaches 195°F (91°C).
5. Rest the pork for 30 minutes before shredding.

NUTRITIONAL FACTS:

540 Kcal, 20g Cho, 35g Fat, 1600mg Na, 48g Pro

RIBS THAT FALL OFF THE BONE UNIQUE BEEF DISHES

SWEET AND SMOKY BABY BACK RIBS

8 SERVINGS   15 MINUTES   240 MINUTES

INSTRUCTIONS:

1. *Remove the membrane from the back of the ribs.*
2. *Mix brown sugar, smoked paprika, salt, garlic powder, onion powder, and black pepper.*
3. *Rub the mixture all over the ribs.*
4. *Preheat your smoker to 225°F (107°C).*
5. *Smoke the ribs for 4 hours, or until tender.*
6. *Optional: Baste with your favorite BBQ sauce in the last 30 minutes.*

INGREDIENTS:

- 2 racks baby back ribs (4 lbs or 1814 g)
- 1/4 cup brown sugar (55 g)
- 2 tbsp smoked paprika (30 g)
- 1 tbsp salt (15 g)
- 1 tbsp garlic powder (15 g)
- 1 tbsp onion powder (15 g)
- 1 tsp black pepper (5 g)

NUTRITIONAL FACTS:

520 Kcal, 10g Cho, 35g Fat, 850mg Na, 40g Pro

STICKY ASIAN PORK RIBS

 8 SERVINGS

 20 MINUTES

 180 MINUTES

NUTRITIONAL FACTS:

630 Kcal, 15g Cho, 40g Fat, 960mg Na, 42g Pro

INSTRUCTIONS:

1. Remove the membrane from the ribs.
2. Mix soy sauce, hoisin sauce, honey, rice vinegar, garlic, ginger, and sesame oil to make the marinade.
3. Marinate the ribs in this mixture for at least 1 hour.
4. Preheat your grill to 300°F (149°C).
5. Grill ribs, covered, for about 3 hours, basting with marinade occasionally.
6. Serve sprinkled with sesame seeds if desired.

INGREDIENTS:

- 2 racks pork ribs (4 lbs or 1814 g)
- 1/4 cup soy sauce (60 ml)
- 1/4 cup hoisin sauce (60 ml)
- 2 tbsp honey (30 ml)
- 2 tbsp rice vinegar (30 ml)
- 4 cloves garlic, minced (16 g)
- 1 tbsp ginger, minced (15 g)
- 1 tsp sesame oil (5 ml)

DRY RUBBED SPARE RIBS WITH APPLE CIDER VINEGAR SPRAY

8 SERVINGS   15 MINUTES   5 HOURS

INSTRUCTIONS:

1. *Mix brown sugar, paprika, black pepper, salt, and cayenne pepper for the dry rub.*
2. *Apply rub generously to the ribs.*
3. *Place ribs in smoker preheated to 225°F (107°C).*
4. *Smoke ribs for 5 hours, spraying with apple cider vinegar hourly.*
5. *Allow ribs to rest for 10 minutes before serving.*

INGREDIENTS:

- 2 racks spare ribs (5 lbs or 2268 g)
- 1/4 cup brown sugar (55 g)
- 2 tbsp paprika (30 g)
- 1 tbsp black pepper (15 g)
- 1 tbsp salt (15 g)
- 1 tsp cayenne pepper (5 g)
- 1 cup apple cider vinegar (240 ml)

NUTRITIONAL FACTS:

490 Kcal, 12g Cho, 32g Fat, 880mg Na, 38g Pro

HONEY-GLAZED ST. LOUIS STYLE RIBS

  8 SERVINGS

  10 MINUTES

  4 HOURS

NUTRITIONAL FACTS:

560 Kcal, 20g Cho, 35g Fat, 1600mg Na, 48g Pro

INSTRUCTIONS:

1. Preheat your smoker to 250°F (121°C).
2. Mix honey, brown sugar, garlic powder, paprika, salt, and pepper.
3. Rub this mixture all over the ribs.
4. Smoke for 4 hours, glazing with additional honey in the last hour.
5. Rest ribs for 10 minutes before serving.

INGREDIENTS:

- 2 racks St. Louis style ribs (4 lbs or 1814 g)
- 2 tbsp honey (30 ml)
- 2 tbsp brown sugar (30 g)
- 1 tbsp garlic powder (15 g)
- 2 tsp paprika (10 g)
- 1 tsp salt (5 g)
- 1 tsp black pepper (5 g)

MEMPHIS STYLE RIBS WITH A SPICY DRY RUB

8 SERVINGS   15 MINUTES   4 HOURS

INSTRUCTIONS:

1. *Combine paprika, garlic powder, onion powder, cumin, salt, black pepper, and cayenne pepper to make the dry rub.*
2. *Rub this mixture all over the ribs thoroughly.*
3. *Smoke the ribs in a smoker set to 225°F (107°C) for about 4 hours.*
4. *Allow ribs to rest for 10 minutes before slicing and serving.*

INGREDIENTS:

- 2 racks pork ribs (4 lbs or 1814 g)
- 3 tbsp paprika (45 g)
- 2 tbsp garlic powder (30 g)
- 1 tbsp onion powder (15 g)
- 1 tbsp ground cumin (15 g)
- 2 tsp salt (10 g)
- 2 tsp black pepper (10 g)
- 1 tsp cayenne pepper (5 g)

NUTRITIONAL FACTS:

540 Kcal, 0g Cho, 35g Fat, 870mg Na, 42g Pro

HONEY-GLAZED ST. LOUIS STYLE RIBS

 8 SERVINGS

 10 MINUTES

 4 HOURS

NUTRITIONAL FACTS:

560 Kcal, 20g Cho, 35g Fat, 1600mg Na, 48g Pro

INSTRUCTIONS:

1. Preheat your smoker to 250°F (121°C).
2. Mix honey, brown sugar, garlic powder, paprika, salt, and pepper.
3. Rub this mixture all over the ribs.
4. Smoke for 4 hours, glazing with additional honey in the last hour.
5. Rest ribs for 10 minutes before serving.

INGREDIENTS:

- 2 racks St. Louis style ribs (4 lbs or 1814 g)
- 2 tbsp honey (30 ml)
- 2 tbsp brown sugar (30 g)
- 1 tbsp garlic powder (15 g)
- 2 tsp paprika (10 g)
- 1 tsp salt (5 g)
- 1 tsp black pepper (5 g)

INNOVATIONS WITH PORK

SMOKED PORK BELLY BURNT ENDS

8 SERVINGS   15 MINUTES   4 HOURS

INSTRUCTIONS:

1. *Preheat your smoker to 250°F (121°C).*
2. *Combine brown sugar, paprika, salt, and pepper in a bowl.*
3. *Toss the pork belly cubes in the spice mix until evenly coated.*
4. *Place pork belly on the smoker rack and smoke for 3 hours.*
5. *Glaze the pork belly with BBQ sauce and continue to smoke for 1 more hour.*
6. *Remove from smoker and serve hot.*

INGREDIENTS:

- 3 lbs pork belly, cubed (1360 g)
- 1/4 cup brown sugar (55 g)
- 2 tbsp smoked paprika (30 g)
- 1 tbsp salt (15 g)
- 1 tbsp black pepper (15 g)
- 1/2 cup BBQ sauce (120 ml)

NUTRITIONAL FACTS:

760 Kcal, 20g Cho, 60g Fat, 900mg Na, 25g Pro

CUBAN MOJO MARINATED PORK SHOULDER

  8 SERVINGS

  20 MINUTES

  180 MINUTES

NUTRITIONAL FACTS:

510 Kcal, 5g Cho, 35g Fat, 950mg Na, 40g Pro

INSTRUCTIONS:

1. Combine orange juice, lime juice, olive oil, garlic, oregano, cumin, salt, and pepper to create the mojo marinade.
2. Marinate the pork shoulder in the mojo marinade overnight in the refrigerator.
3. Preheat your smoker to 225°F (107°C).
4. Smoke the marinated pork shoulder for about 6 hours or until tender.
5. Let rest for 30 minutes before shredding.

INGREDIENTS:

- 5 lbs pork shoulder (2268 g)
- 1 cup orange juice (240 ml)
- 1/4 cup lime juice (60 ml)
- 1/4 cup olive oil (60 ml)
- 6 cloves garlic, minced (24 g)
- 1 tbsp oregano (15 g)
- 1 tbsp cumin (15 g)
- 1 tbsp salt (15 g)
- 2 tsp black pepper (10 g)

PORK CHOPS WITH APPLE AND CINNAMON

8 SERVINGS   10 MINUTES   15 MINUTES

INGREDIENTS:

- 8 pork chops, bone-in (3 lbs or 1360 g)
- 2 apples, sliced (300 g)
- 2 tbsp cinnamon (30 g)
- 2 tbsp brown sugar (30 g)
- 1 tbsp butter (15 g)

INSTRUCTIONS:

1. *Preheat grill to medium-high, about 375°F (190°C).*
2. *Season pork chops with cinnamon and brown sugar.*
3. *Grill pork chops for 7 minutes on each side or until fully cooked.*
4. *In a pan, sauté apple slices in butter until soft.*
5. *Serve pork chops topped with sautéed apples.*

NUTRITIONAL FACTS:

350 Kcal, 10g Cho, 18g Fat, 85mg Na, 30g Pro

THAI STYLE PORK SKEWERS

 8 SERVINGS

 25 MINUTES

 10 MINUTES

 NUTRITIONAL FACTS:

210 Kcal, 5g Cho, 6g Fat, 680mg Na, 32g Pro

INGREDIENTS:

- 2 lbs pork tenderloin, thinly sliced (907 g)
- 1/4 cup soy sauce (60 ml)
- 2 tbsp fish sauce (30 ml)
- 2 tbsp lime juice (30 ml)
- 2 tbsp brown sugar (30 g)
- 3 cloves garlic, minced (12 g)
- 1 tbsp grated ginger (15 g)
- 1 tsp red pepper flakes (5 g)

INSTRUCTIONS:

1. Combine soy sauce, fish sauce, lime juice, brown sugar, garlic, ginger, and red pepper flakes to make a marinade.
2. Marinate the pork slices for 15 minutes.
3. Thread the pork onto skewers.
4. Preheat grill to high, about 450°F (232°C).
5. Grill skewers for 5 minutes on each side or until cooked through.

GERMAN SMOKED PORK KNUCKLE

8 SERVINGS   10 MINUTES   4 HOURS

INGREDIENTS:

- 4 pork knuckles (8 lbs or 3629 g)
- 1 tbsp salt (15 g)
- 2 tsp black pepper (10 g)
- 2 onions, quartered (300 g)
- 4 cloves garlic (16 g)
- 1 liter beer (1000 ml)

INSTRUCTIONS:

1. Rub pork knuckles with salt and pepper.
2. Place onions and garlic in the bottom of a smoker tray.
3. Set pork knuckles over the onions and garlic.
4. Pour beer into the tray.
5. Smoke at 275°F (135°C) for 4 hours or until the skin is crispy and meat is tender.
6. Serve pork knuckles with sauerkraut or potatoes.

NUTRITIONAL FACTS:

890 Kcal, 5g Cho, 68g Fat, 950mg Na, 60g Pro

SMOKED SAUSAGE AND PEPPERS

 8 SERVINGS

 10 MINUTES

 1 HOUR

NUTRITIONAL FACTS:

290 Kcal, 5g Cho, 23g Fat, 680mg Na, 15g Pro

INSTRUCTIONS:

1. Preheat your smoker to 250°F (121°C).
2. Toss sausage, peppers, and onion with olive oil, salt, and pepper.
3. Place the mixture in a large disposable aluminum tray.
4. Smoke for 1 hour, stirring occasionally, until the vegetables are tender and the sausage is heated through.
5. Serve hot.

INGREDIENTS:

- 2 lbs smoked sausage, sliced (907 g)
- 2 red bell peppers, sliced (300 g)
- 2 green bell peppers, sliced (300 g)
- 1 large onion, sliced (150 g)
- 2 tbsp olive oil (30 ml)
- 1 tsp salt (5 g)
- 1 tsp black pepper (5 g)

SMOKED HAM WITH BROWN SUGAR GLAZE

8 SERVINGS   15 MINUTES   3 HOURS

INSTRUCTIONS:

1. *Preheat your smoker to 225°F (107°C).*
2. *Score the surface of the ham in a diamond pattern.*
3. *Place the ham in the smoker.*
4. *Combine brown sugar, honey, Dijon mustard, and pineapple juice in a bowl to make the glaze.*
5. *Brush the ham with the glaze every 30 minutes.*
6. *Smoke until the internal temperature reaches 140°F (60°C).*
7. *Let the ham rest for 10 minutes before slicing.*

INGREDIENTS:

- 1 whole ham, bone-in (8 lbs or 3629 g)
- 1 cup brown sugar (220 g)
- 1/4 cup honey (60 ml)
- 1/4 cup Dijon mustard (60 ml)
- 1/2 cup pineapple juice (120 ml)

NUTRITIONAL FACTS:

890 Kcal, 30g Cho, 40g Fat, 1400mg Na, 80g Pro

SMOKED PORCINI MUSHROOM AND PORK BURGERS

 8 SERVINGS

 20 MINUTES

 1 HOUR

NUTRITIONAL FACTS:

320 Kcal, 5g Cho, 20g Fat, 650mg Na, 28g Pro

INSTRUCTIONS:

1. Preheat your smoker to 225°F (107°C).
2. In a bowl, mix ground pork, porcini mushrooms, breadcrumbs, onion, garlic, Worcestershire sauce, salt, and pepper.
3. Form the mixture into 8 patties.
4. Smoke the patties for 1 hour or until fully cooked.
5. Serve on burger buns with your favorite toppings.

INGREDIENTS:

- 2 lbs ground pork (907 g)
- 1 cup porcini mushrooms, finely chopped (70 g)
- 1/4 cup breadcrumbs (30 g)
- 1 onion, finely chopped (150 g)
- 2 cloves garlic, minced (8 g)
- 2 tbsp Worcestershire sauce (30 ml)
- Salt and pepper to taste

ITALIAN PORCHETTA WITH CRISPY SKIN

8 SERVINGS   20 MINUTES   4 HOURS

INGREDIENTS:

- 5 lbs pork belly with skin (2268 g)
- 1/4 cup fresh rosemary, chopped (15 g)
- 1/4 cup fresh sage, chopped (15 g)
- 4 cloves garlic, minced (16 g)
- 2 tbsp fennel seeds (30 g)
- 2 tbsp salt (30 g)
- 1 tbsp black pepper (15 g)

INSTRUCTIONS:

1. *Score the pork skin in a crosshatch pattern.*
2. *Rub the inside of the pork belly with rosemary, sage, garlic, fennel seeds, salt, and pepper.*
3. *Roll up the pork belly tightly and tie it with kitchen twine.*
4. *Preheat your smoker to 300°F (149°C).*
5. *Smoke for 4 hours or until the skin is crispy and the meat is tender.*
6. *Let rest for 20 minutes before slicing.*

NUTRITIONAL FACTS:

880 Kcal, 1g Cho, 80g Fat, 1800mg Na, 40g Pro

CAJUN ANDOUILLE SAUSAGE LINKS

   8 SERVINGS

   10 MINUTES

   1 HOUR

NUTRITIONAL FACTS:

320 Kcal, 1g Cho, 28g Fat, 1100mg Na, 19g Pro

INGREDIENTS:

- 2 lbs Andouille sausage links (907 g)
- 1 tbsp Cajun seasoning (15 g)

INSTRUCTIONS:

1. Preheat your smoker to 250°F (121°C).
2. Sprinkle Cajun seasoning evenly over the sausage links.
3. Place the sausages in the smoker.
4. Smoke for 1 hour or until the sausages are cooked through.
5. Serve hot, sliced or whole, with your favorite side dishes.

PORK TENDERLOIN WITH PEACH BBQ SAUCE

8 SERVINGS   15 MINUTES   45 MINUTES

INSTRUCTIONS:

1. *Preheat grill to medium-high, about 350°F (177°C).*
2. *Rub pork tenderloins with olive oil, garlic powder, onion powder, smoked paprika, salt, and pepper.*
3. *Grill tenderloins for about 20 minutes, turning occasionally.*
4. *Mix peach preserves and apple cider vinegar to make the BBQ sauce.*
5. *Brush sauce over pork in the last 10 minutes of grilling.*
6. *Let pork rest for 10 minutes before slicing.*

INGREDIENTS:

- 2 pork tenderloins (2 lbs or 907 g)
- 1 cup peach preserves (240 ml)
- 2 tbsp apple cider vinegar (30 ml)
- 1 tbsp olive oil (15 ml)
- 1 tsp garlic powder (5 g)
- 1 tsp onion powder (5 g)
- 1 tsp smoked paprika (5 g)
- Salt and pepper to taste

NUTRITIONAL FACTS:

250 Kcal, 20g Cho, 8g Fat, 55mg Na, 24g Pro

SZECHUAN SMOKED PORK WITH HOISIN SAUCE

 8 SERVINGS

 10 MINUTES

 3 HOURS

NUTRITIONAL FACTS:

310 Kcal, 10g Cho, 18g Fat, 500mg Na, 28g Pro

INSTRUCTIONS:

1. Preheat your smoker to 250°F (121°C).
2. Mix hoisin sauce, soy sauce, honey, Szechuan peppercorns, garlic, and ginger in a bowl.
3. Rub the mixture over the pork chunks.
4. Smoke for about 3 hours or until tender.
5. Serve the pork with additional hoisin sauce if desired.

INGREDIENTS:

- 3 lbs pork shoulder, cut into large chunks (1360 g)
- 1/4 cup hoisin sauce (60 ml)
- 2 tbsp soy sauce (30 ml)
- 2 tbsp honey (30 ml)
- 1 tbsp Szechuan peppercorns, crushed (15 g)
- 3 cloves garlic, minced (12 g)
- 1 tbsp ginger, minced (15 g)

CHORIZO STUFFED SMOKED POBLANOS

8 SERVINGS   15 MINUTES   1 HOUR

INGREDIENTS:

- 8 large poblano peppers (800 g)
- 1 lb chorizo, cooked and crumbled (453 g)
- 1 cup cream cheese, softened (240 g)
- 1/2 cup cheddar cheese, shredded (60 g)
- 1/4 cup cilantro, chopped (15 g)

INSTRUCTIONS:

1. *Preheat your smoker to 225°F (107°C).*
2. *Slice the poblanos lengthwise and remove seeds.*
3. *Mix chorizo, cream cheese, cheddar cheese, and cilantro in a bowl.*
4. *Stuff the poblanos with the chorizo mixture.*
5. *Smoke for 1 hour or until the peppers are tender.*
6. *Serve warm.*

NUTRITIONAL FACTS:

400 Kcal, 5g Cho, 30g Fat, 850mg Na, 22g Pro

GRILLED PORK BANH MI SANDWICHES

  8 SERVINGS

10 MINUTES

1 HOUR

NUTRITIONAL FACTS:

450 Kcal, 40g Cho, 15g Fat, 850mg Na, 35g Pro

INGREDIENTS:

- 2 lbs pork tenderloin, thinly sliced (907 g)
- 1/4 cup soy sauce (60 ml)
- 2 tbsp fish sauce (30 ml)
- 2 tbsp sugar (30 g)
- 4 cloves garlic, minced (16 g)
- 1 baguette, sliced into 8 pieces (450 g)
- 1 cucumber, sliced (150 g)
- 1 carrot, julienned (100 g)
- 1/4 cup cilantro leaves (15 g)
- 1 jalapeño, sliced (25 g)

INSTRUCTIONS:

1. Marinate pork slices in soy sauce, fish sauce, sugar, and garlic for 20 minutes.
2. Preheat grill to medium-high, about 350°F (177°C).
3. Grill pork until cooked through, about 5 minutes per side.
4. Assemble sandwiches with pork, cucumber, carrot, cilantro, and jalapeño in baguette slices.

SMOKED MAPLE AND MUSTARD PORK LOIN

8 SERVINGS

15 MINUTES

3 HOURS

INSTRUCTIONS:

1. *Preheat your smoker to 225°F (107°C).*
2. *Mix maple syrup, Dijon mustard, apple cider vinegar, garlic, salt, and pepper.*
3. *Rub the mixture all over the pork loin.*
4. *Smoke for about 3 hours or until the internal temperature reaches 145°F (63°C).*
5. *Let rest for 10 minutes before slicing.*

INGREDIENTS:

- 3 lbs pork loin (1360 g)
- 1/4 cup maple syrup (60 ml)
- 1/4 cup Dijon mustard (60 ml)
- 2 tbsp apple cider vinegar (30 ml)
- 2 cloves garlic, minced (8 g)
- Salt and pepper to taste

NUTRITIONAL FACTS:

310 Kcal, 10g Cho, 10g Fat, 290mg Na, 40g Pro

CHAPTER 6: POULTRY AND MORE

SMOKY GRILLED CHICKEN

BASIC SMOKED WHOLE CHICKEN

8 SERVINGS

15 MINUTES

3 HOURS

INSTRUCTIONS:

1. Preheat your smoker to 250°F (121°C).
2. Rub the chicken all over with olive oil.
3. Combine salt, black pepper, and smoked paprika, then season the chicken inside and out.
4. Place the chicken in the smoker.
5. Smoke for about 3 hours or until the internal temperature reaches 165°F (74°C).
6. Let the chicken rest for 10 minutes before carving.

INGREDIENTS:

- 1 whole chicken (4 lbs or 1814 g)
- 2 tbsp olive oil (30 ml)
- 1 tbsp salt (15 g)
- 1 tbsp black pepper (15 g)
- 1 tbsp smoked paprika (15 g)

NUTRITIONAL FACTS:

310 Kcal, 0g Cho, 20g Fat, 590mg Na, 30g Pro

LEMON PEPPER CHICKEN THIGHS

8 SERVINGS

10 MINUTES

40 MINUTES

NUTRITIONAL FACTS:

420 Kcal, 1g Cho, 32g Fat, 600mg Na, 31g Pro

INSTRUCTIONS:

1. Preheat grill to medium-high, about 375°F (190°C).
2. In a bowl, mix lemon juice, zest, olive oil, black pepper, and salt.
3. Coat chicken thighs evenly with the lemon pepper mixture.
4. Grill chicken thighs for 20 minutes per side, or until the internal temperature reaches 165°F (74°C).
5. Serve hot.

INGREDIENTS:

- 8 chicken thighs, bone-in, skin-on (3 lbs or 1360 g)
- 2 lemons, juiced and zested (100 ml juice, 10 g zest)
- 1/4 cup olive oil (60 ml)
- 1 tbsp black pepper (15 g)
- 2 tsp salt (10 g)

BBQ CHICKEN DRUMSTICKS

8 SERVINGS   10 MINUTES   45 MINUTES

INGREDIENTS:

- 16 chicken drumsticks (4 lbs or 1814 g)
- 1 cup BBQ sauce (240 ml)
- 2 tbsp honey (30 ml)
- 1 tbsp paprika (15 g)
- 1 tsp garlic powder (5 g)
- Salt and pepper to taste

INSTRUCTIONS:

1. *Preheat your grill to medium, about 350°F (177°C).*
2. *Season drumsticks with paprika, garlic powder, salt, and pepper.*
3. *Grill drumsticks for 35 minutes, turning occasionally.*
4. *Mix BBQ sauce and honey in a bowl.*
5. *Brush the sauce mixture over the drumsticks in the last 10 minutes of grilling.*
6. *Cook until the sauce is caramelized and chicken is fully cooked.*

NUTRITIONAL FACTS:

380 Kcal, 15g Cho, 20g Fat, 590mg Na, 35g Pro

THAI SPICED CHICKEN WINGS

  8 SERVINGS

  20 MINUTES

  30 MINUTES

NUTRITIONAL FACTS:

290 Kcal, 5g Cho, 20g Fat, 850mg Na, 22g Pro

INGREDIENTS:

- 3 lbs chicken wings (1360 g)
- 1/4 cup soy sauce (60 ml)
- 1/4 cup fish sauce (60 ml)
- 2 tbsp brown sugar (30 g)
- 1 tbsp chili flakes (15 g)
- 4 cloves garlic, minced (16 g)
- 1 tbsp ginger, minced (15 g)

INSTRUCTIONS:

1. Combine soy sauce, fish sauce, brown sugar, chili flakes, garlic, and ginger in a bowl.
2. Marinate the chicken wings in the mixture for 15 minutes.
3. Preheat your grill to high, about 450°F (232°C).
4. Grill the wings for 15 minutes per side, until crispy and fully cooked.
5. Serve hot with extra sauce if desired.

MOROCCAN CHICKEN KEBABS

8 SERVINGS   25 MINUTES   15 MINUTES

INGREDIENTS:

- 2 lbs chicken breast, cubed (907 g)
- 2 tbsp olive oil (30 ml)
- 2 tbsp lemon juice (30 ml)
- 1 tbsp cumin (15 g)
- 1 tbsp paprika (15 g)
- 1 tsp turmeric (5 g)
- 1 tsp cinnamon (5 g)
- Salt and pepper to taste

NUTRITIONAL FACTS:

: 210 Kcal, 2g Cho, 10g Fat, 450mg Na, 29g Pro

INSTRUCTIONS:

1. *In a bowl, combine olive oil, lemon juice, cumin, paprika, turmeric, cinnamon, salt, and pepper.*
2. *Add chicken cubes to the marinade and let sit for 15 minutes.*
3. *Thread chicken onto skewers.*
4. *Preheat grill to medium-high, about 375°F (190°C).*
5. *Grill skewers for 7-8 minutes on each side or until fully cooked.*
6. *Serve hot, garnished with fresh cilantro if desired.*

THANKSGIVING TURKEY ON THE GRILL

CLASSIC SMOKED TURKEY WITH HERBED BUTTER

8 SERVINGS   30 MINUTES   4 HOURS

INSTRUCTIONS:

1. *Preheat your smoker to 225°F (107°C).*
2. *Mix butter with rosemary, thyme, and sage.*
3. *Loosen the skin of the turkey and spread the herbed butter under and on the skin.*
4. *Season the turkey inside and out with salt and pepper.*
5. *Place the turkey in the smoker.*
6. *Smoke for about 4 hours, or until the internal temperature reaches 165°F (74°C).*
7. *Rest for 20 minutes before carving.*

INGREDIENTS:

- 1 whole turkey (12 lbs or 5443 g)
- 1/2 cup unsalted butter, softened (113 g)
- 2 tbsp fresh rosemary, minced (30 g)
- 2 tbsp fresh thyme, minced (30 g)
- 2 tbsp fresh sage, minced (30 g)
- Salt and pepper to taste

NUTRITIONAL FACTS:

670 Kcal, 0g Cho, 40g Fat, 620mg Na, 70g Pro

CAJUN SPICED TURKEY

 8 SERVINGS

 20 MINUTES

 4 HOURS

NUTRITIONAL FACTS:

630 Kcal, 0g Cho, 35g Fat, 880mg Na, 75g Pro

INSTRUCTIONS:

1. Preheat your smoker to 250°F (121°C).
2. Rub the turkey with olive oil.
3. Combine Cajun seasoning, garlic powder, and onion powder.
4. Season the turkey thoroughly with the spice mix.
5. Place the turkey in the smoker.
6. Smoke for about 4 hours, or until the internal temperature reaches 165°F (74°C).
7. Allow the turkey to rest before slicing.

INGREDIENTS:

- 1 whole turkey (10 lbs or 4536 g)
- 3 tbsp Cajun seasoning (45 g)
- 1 tbsp garlic powder (15 g)
- 1 tbsp onion powder (15 g)
- 2 tbsp olive oil (30 ml)

APPLEWOOD SMOKED TURKEY WITH CIDER GLAZE

8 SERVINGS   25 MINUTES   4 HOURS

INSTRUCTIONS:

1. *Preheat your smoker to 225°F (107°C).*
2. *Mix apple cider, honey, mustard, and vinegar to create the glaze.*
3. *Rub the turkey with olive oil, salt, and pepper.*
4. *Smoke the turkey for 3 hours, then start basting with the cider glaze every 30 minutes.*
5. *Continue to smoke until the internal temperature reaches 165°F (74°C).*
6. *Let the turkey rest before carving.*

INGREDIENTS:

- 1 whole turkey (12 lbs or 5443 g)
- 1 cup apple cider (240 ml)
- 1/4 cup honey (60 ml)
- 1/4 cup Dijon mustard (60 ml)
- 2 tbsp apple cider vinegar (30 ml)
- 2 tbsp olive oil (30 ml)
- Salt and pepper to taste

NUTRITIONAL FACTS:

710 Kcal, 15g Cho, 40g Fat, 700mg Na, 80g Pro

HICKORY SMOKED TURKEY WITH CRANBERRY RELISH

 8 SERVINGS

NUTRITIONAL FACTS:

650 Kcal, 20g Cho, 30g Fat, 620mg Na, 70g Pro

 20 MINUTES

 4 HOURS

INSTRUCTIONS:

1. Preheat your smoker to 225°F (107°C).
2. Season the turkey with salt and pepper.
3. Place the turkey in the smoker.
4. Cook for about 4 hours, or until the internal temperature reaches 165°F (74°C).
5. For the relish, combine cranberries, orange zest, orange juice, and sugar in a saucepan.
6. Cook over medium heat until the cranberries burst and the mixture thickens.
7. Serve the turkey with cranberry relish.

INGREDIENTS:

- 1 whole turkey (12 lbs or 5443 g)
- Salt and pepper to taste
- For the relish:
- 2 cups fresh cranberries (200 g)
- 1 orange, zested and juiced (120 ml juice, 5 g zest)
- 1/2 cup sugar (100 g)

SPATCHCOCK TURKEY WITH LEMON AND SAGE

8 SERVINGS

20 INUTES

3 HOURS

INGREDIENTS:

- 8 large poblano peppers (800 g)
- 1 lb chorizo, cooked and crumbled (453 g)
- 1 cup cream cheese, softened (240 g)
- 1/2 cup cheddar cheese, shredded (60 g)
- 1/4 cup cilantro, chopped (15 g)

INSTRUCTIONS:

1. *Preheat your smoker to 325°F (163°C).*
2. *Rub the turkey all over with olive oil.*
3. *Mix lemon zest, lemon juice, and chopped sage.*
4. *Season the turkey liberally with the lemon-sage mixture, salt, and pepper.*
5. *Place the turkey in the smoker.*
6. *Smoke for about 3 hours, or until the internal temperature reaches 165°F (74°C).*
7. *Rest the turkey for 20 minutes before carving.*
8. *Nutritional Information: 690 Kcal, 1g Cho, 40g Fat, 630mg Na, 80g Pro*

NUTRITIONAL FACTS:

400 Kcal, 5g Cho, 30g Fat, 850mg Na, 22g Pro

EXOTIC BIRD RECIPES

SMOKED DUCK WITH ORANGE GLAZE

8 SERVINGS   20 MINUTES   3 HOURS

INSTRUCTIONS:

1. *Preheat your smoker to 250°F (121°C).*
2. *Season the duck with salt and pepper.*
3. *Place the duck in the smoker.*
4. *Mix orange juice, honey, soy sauce, and orange zest in a bowl to make the glaze.*
5. *Baste the duck with the glaze every 30 minutes.*
6. *Smoke until the internal temperature reaches 165°F (74°C).*
7. *Allow the duck to rest before serving.*

INGREDIENTS:

- 1 whole duck (4 lbs or 1814 g)
- 1 cup orange juice (240 ml)
- 1/4 cup honey (60 ml)
- 2 tbsp soy sauce (30 ml)
- 1 orange, zested (10 g)
- Salt and pepper to taste

NUTRITIONAL FACTS:

450 Kcal, 20g Cho, 30g Fat, 650mg Na, 35g Pro

PEKING STYLE SMOKED DUCK

 8 SERVINGS

 24 HOURS

 3 HOURS

NUTRITIONAL FACTS:

630 Kcal, 0g Cho, 35g Fat, 880mg Na, 75g Pro

INSTRUCTIONS:

1. Mix hoisin sauce, honey, soy sauce, garlic, ginger, and five-spice powder in a bowl.
2. Rub the mixture inside and outside the duck.
3. Let the duck marinate in the refrigerator for 24 hours.
4. Preheat your smoker to 250°F (121°C).
5. Smoke the duck for 3 hours.
6. Let rest before slicing.

INGREDIENTS:

- 1 whole duck (4 lbs or 1814 g)
- 1/4 cup hoisin sauce (60 ml)
- 2 tbsp honey (30 ml)
- 2 tbsp soy sauce (30 ml)
- 2 cloves garlic, minced (8 g)
- 1 piece ginger, grated (10 g)
- 1 tbsp five-spice powder (15 g)

GRILLED QUAIL WITH BALSAMIC REDUCTION

8 SERVINGS   10 MINUTES   20 MINUTES

INSTRUCTIONS:

1. *Preheat grill to medium-high, about 375°F (190°C).*
2. *Season quails with salt and pepper.*
3. *Grill quails for 10 minutes per side or until fully cooked.*
4. *Simmer balsamic vinegar, honey, and rosemary in a saucepan until reduced by half.*
5. *Drizzle the reduction over grilled quails before serving.*

INGREDIENTS:

- 8 quails (1600 g)
- 1 cup balsamic vinegar (240 ml)
- 2 tbsp honey (30 ml)
- 1 tbsp rosemary, minced (15 g)
- Salt and pepper to taste

NUTRITIONAL FACTS:

300 Kcal, 10g Cho, 15g Fat, 400mg Na, 30g Pro

JERK SEASONED SMOKED CORNISH HENS

 8 SERVINGS

NUTRITIONAL FACTS:

410 Kcal, 0g Cho, 31g Fat, 700mg Na, 35g Pro

 15 MINUTES

 2 HOURS

INSTRUCTIONS:

1. Rub each hen half with olive oil and jerk seasoning.
2. Preheat your smoker to 275°F (135°C).
3. Place the hens in the smoker.
4. Smoke for 2 hours or until the internal temperature reaches 165°F (74°C).
5. Serve hot with your choice of side.

INGREDIENTS:

- 4 Cornish hens, halved (8 lbs or 3629 g)
- 3 tbsp jerk seasoning (45 g)
- 1 tbsp olive oil (15 ml)
- Salt to taste

TEQUILA LIME SMOKED TURKEY LEGS

8 SERVINGS

30 MINUTES

4 HOURS

INSTRUCTIONS:

1. Mix tequila, lime juice, salt, chili powder, and garlic powder in a bowl.
2. Rub the mixture over the turkey legs.
3. Preheat your smoker to 225°F (107°C).
4. Smoke the turkey legs for about 4 hours or until the meat is tender and pulls away from the bone.
5. Baste occasionally with the tequila lime mixture.

INGREDIENTS:

- 8 turkey legs (6 lbs or 2722 g)
- 1/2 cup tequila (120 ml)
- 1/4 cup lime juice (60 ml)
- 2 tbsp salt (30 g)
- 2 tbsp chili powder (30 g)
- 1 tbsp garlic powder (15 g)

NUTRITIONAL FACTS:

540 Kcal, 0g Cho, 24g Fat, 1500mg Na, 70g Pro

SMOKED GOOSE WITH APPLE STUFFING

8 SERVINGS

30 MINUTES

4 HOURS

NUTRITIONAL FACTS:

950 Kcal, 20g Cho, 70g Fat, 1800mg Na, 50g Pro

INSTRUCTIONS:

1. Preheat your smoker to 225°F (107°C).
2. Mix apples, breadcrumbs, onion, celery, butter, salt, and pepper to make the stuffing.
3. Stuff the goose with the apple mixture.
4. Truss the goose and place it in the smoker.
5. Smoke for about 4 hours or until the internal temperature reaches 165°F (74°C).
6. Let the goose rest for 20 minutes before carving.

INGREDIENTS:

- 1 whole goose (10 lbs or 4536 g)
- 3 apples, diced (450 g)
- 1 cup breadcrumbs (120 g)
- 1 onion, diced (150 g)
- 2 celery stalks, diced (100 g)
- 1/4 cup melted butter (60 ml)
- 2 tsp salt (10 g)
- 1 tsp black pepper (5 g)

GRILLED PHEASANT WITH JUNIPER BERRIES

8 SERVINGS   15 MINUTES   40 MINUTES

INSTRUCTIONS:

1. *Marinate pheasant pieces in gin, crushed juniper berries, olive oil, rosemary, salt, and pepper for at least 1 hour.*
2. *Preheat grill to medium-high, about 375°F (190°C).*
3. *Grill pheasant pieces for 20 minutes per side or until fully cooked.*
4. *Serve hot, garnished with additional rosemary if desired.*

INGREDIENTS:

- 2 whole pheasants, quartered (5 lbs or 2268 g)
- 1/4 cup gin (60 ml)
- 2 tbsp juniper berries, crushed (30 g)
- 2 tbsp olive oil (30 ml)
- 1 tbsp rosemary, chopped (15 g)
- Salt and pepper to taste

NUTRITIONAL FACTS:

310 Kcal, 1g Cho, 12g Fat, 650mg Na, 48g Pro

SMOKED PARTRIDGE WITH WILD BERRY SAUCE

 8 SERVINGS

 20 MINUTES

 2 HOURS

NUTRITIONAL FACTS:

420 Kcal, 11g Cho, 10g Fat, 300mg Na, 60g Pro

INSTRUCTIONS:

1. Preheat your smoker to 225°F (107°C).
2. Season partridges with salt and pepper.
3. Place in the smoker and cook for about 2 hours.
4. Simmer wild berries, red wine, honey, and balsamic vinegar in a saucepan until reduced to a thick sauce.
5. Serve the smoked partridges with the berry sauce drizzled over the top.

INGREDIENTS:

- 4 partridges (4 lbs or 1814 g)
- 1 cup mixed wild berries (150 g)
- 1/2 cup red wine (120 ml)
- 2 tbsp honey (30 ml)
- 1 tbsp balsamic vinegar (15 ml)
- Salt and pepper to taste

BARBECUE PIGEON WITH SWEET AND SPICY RUB

8 SERVINGS   10 MINUTES   30 MINUTES

INSTRUCTIONS:

1. *Mix brown sugar, chili powder, garlic powder, cayenne pepper, salt, and pepper to create a rub.*
2. *Rub the mixture all over the pigeons.*
3. *Preheat grill to medium-high, about 375°F (190°C).*
4. *Grill pigeons for 15 minutes per side or until the skin is crispy and meat is cooked.*
5. *Serve hot.*

INGREDIENTS:

- 8 pigeons (6 lbs or 2722 g)
- 2 tbsp brown sugar (30 g)
- 1 tbsp chili powder (15 g)
- 1 tsp garlic powder (5 g)
- 1 tsp cayenne pepper (5 g)
- Salt and pepper to taste

NUTRITIONAL FACTS:

350 Kcal, 5g Cho, 10g Fat, 500mg Na, 58g Pro

GRILLED EMU STEAKS WITH PEPPERBERRY RUB

 8 SERVINGS

 10 MINUTES

 15 MINUTES

NUTRITIONAL FACTS:

290 Kcal, 0g Cho, 15g Fat, 450mg Na, 38g Pro

INSTRUCTIONS:

1. Combine ground pepperberry, salt, and thyme.
2. Rub the spice mix and olive oil over the emu steaks.
3. Preheat grill to high, about 450°F (232°C).
4. Grill steaks for about 7-8 minutes per side or until desired doneness is reached.
5. Serve steaks with a side of grilled vegetables.

INGREDIENTS:

- 8 emu steaks (4 lbs or 1814 g)
- 2 tbsp ground pepper-berry (30 g)
- 1 tbsp salt (15 g)
- 2 tsp dried thyme (10 g)
- 2 tbsp olive oil (30 ml)

HONEY-SESAME SMOKED CHICKEN BREAST

8 SERVINGS   15 MINUTES   90 MINUTES

INGREDIENTS:

- 4 chicken breasts, boneless and skinless (2 lbs or 907 g)
- 1/4 cup honey (60 ml)
- 2 tbsp soy sauce (30 ml)
- 2 tbsp sesame oil (30 ml)
- 1 tbsp sesame seeds (15 g)
- 1 tsp garlic powder (5 g)
- Salt and pepper to taste

INSTRUCTIONS:

1. *Preheat your smoker to 250°F (121°C).*
2. *Whisk together honey, soy sauce, sesame oil, and garlic powder.*
3. *Season chicken breasts with salt and pepper, then coat with the honey mixture.*
4. *Place chicken in the smoker and cook for about 1 hour 30 minutes.*
5. *Sprinkle sesame seeds over the chicken in the last 10 minutes of cooking.*
6. *Remove from smoker and let rest before serving.*

NUTRITIONAL FACTS:

230 Kcal, 10g Cho, 9g Fat, 400mg Na, 29g Pro

GRILLED OSTRICH FILLETS WITH RED WINE SAUCE

 8 SERVINGS

 10 MINUTES

 20 MINUTES

NUTRITIONAL FACTS:

360 Kcal, 2g Cho, 10g Fat, 620mg Na, 60g Pro

INGREDIENTS:

- 8 ostrich fillets (4 lbs or 1814 g)
- 1 cup red wine (240 ml)
- 1/4 cup balsamic vinegar (60 ml)
- 2 tbsp olive oil (30 ml)
- 1 tbsp rosemary, minced (15 g)
- Salt and pepper to taste

INSTRUCTIONS:

1. Preheat grill to high, about 450°F (232°C).
2. Season ostrich fillets with salt, pepper, and rosemary.
3. Grill fillets for 5 minutes per side or until desired doneness.
4. Simultaneously, reduce red wine and balsamic vinegar in a saucepan over medium heat until thickened.
5. Serve fillets with the red wine sauce drizzled over the top.

SMOKED TURKEY BREAST WITH MAPLE SYRUP GLAZE

8 SERVINGS   15 MINUTES   3 HOURS

INGREDIENTS:

- 1 whole turkey breast (6 lbs or 2722 g)
- 1/2 cup maple syrup (120 ml)
- 2 tbsp Dijon mustard (30 ml)
- 1 tbsp apple cider vinegar (15 ml)
- Salt and pepper to taste

INSTRUCTIONS:

1. *Preheat your smoker to 225°F (107°C).*
2. *Season the turkey breast with salt and pepper.*
3. *Mix maple syrup, Dijon mustard, and apple cider vinegar to make the glaze.*
4. *Smoke the turkey, brushing with glaze every 30 minutes.*
5. *Cook until the internal temperature reaches 165°F (74°C).*
6. *Let rest before slicing.*

NUTRITIONAL FACTS:

280 Kcal, 10g Cho, 4g Fat, 350mg Na, 44g Pro

HERB-SMOKED CHICKEN SKEWERS

 8 SERVINGS

 20 MINUTES

 30 MINUTES

NUTRITIONAL FACTS:

220 Kcal, 1g Cho, 10g Fat, 300mg Na, 29g Pro

INGREDIENTS:

- 2 lbs chicken breast, cubed (907 g)
- 1/4 cup olive oil (60 ml)
- 1/4 cup lemon juice (60 ml)
- 1 tbsp fresh rosemary, minced (15 g)
- 1 tbsp fresh thyme, minced (15 g)
- 1 tbsp garlic, minced (15 g)
- Salt and pepper to taste

INSTRUCTIONS:

1. In a bowl, mix olive oil, lemon juice, rosemary, thyme, garlic, salt, and pepper.
2. Marinate chicken cubes in the herb mixture for 15 minutes.
3. Thread chicken onto skewers.
4. Preheat your smoker to 250°F (121°C).
5. Smoke skewers for 30 minutes or until cooked through.
6. Serve hot.

SPICED SMOKED CHICKEN WITH YOGURT DIP

8 SERVINGS   20 MINUTES   90 MINUTES

INGREDIENTS:

- 2 lbs chicken thighs, boneless and skinless (907 g)
- 1 tbsp paprika (15 g)
- 1 tbsp cumin (15 g)
- 1 tsp cayenne pepper (5 g)
- 1 cup plain yogurt (240 ml)
- 2 tbsp mint, chopped (30 g)
- 1 cucumber, finely diced (150 g)
- Salt and pepper to taste

INSTRUCTIONS:

1. *Combine paprika, cumin, cayenne pepper, salt, and pepper; rub onto the chicken thighs.*
2. *Preheat your smoker to 250°F (121°C).*
3. *Smoke the chicken thighs for about 1 hour 30 minutes.*
4. *Mix yogurt, mint, and cucumber to make the dip.*
5. *Serve the smoked chicken with the yogurt dip on the side.*

NUTRITIONAL FACTS:

210 Kcal, 5g Cho, 10g Fat, 620mg Na, 28g Pro

CHAPTER 7: FISH AND SEAFOOD

SMOKED SALMON SECRETS

CLASSIC SMOKED SALMON

8 SERVINGS   10 MINUTES   3 HOURS

INSTRUCTIONS:

1. *Mix salt, sugar, and black pepper together.*
2. *Rub the mixture over the salmon fillet.*
3. *Let the salmon cure in the refrigerator for 2 hours.*
4. *Preheat your smoker to 225°F (107°C).*
5. *Smoke the salmon for 3 hours.*
6. *Slice thinly to serve.*

INGREDIENTS:

- 2 lbs salmon fillet (907 g)
- 1/4 cup salt (60 g)
- 1/4 cup sugar (55 g)
- 1 tbsp black pepper (15 g)

NUTRITIONAL FACTS:

200 Kcal, 0g Cho, 12g Fat, 1500mg Na, 23g Pro

HONEY DIJON SMOKED SALMON

 8 SERVINGS

 10 MINUTES

 3 HOURS

NUTRITIONAL FACTS:

210 Kcal, 5g Cho, 8g Fat, 650mg Na, 23g Pro

INSTRUCTIONS:

1. Preheat your smoker to 225°F (107°C).
2. Mix honey and Dijon mustard in a bowl.
3. Season the salmon with salt and pepper.
4. Glaze the salmon with the honey mustard mixture.
5. Smoke for 3 hours or until cooked through.
6. Slice and serve.

INGREDIENTS:

- 2 lbs salmon fillet (907 g)
- 1/4 cup honey (60 ml)
- 2 tbsp Dijon mustard (30 ml)
- Salt and pepper to taste

MAPLE GLAZED SMOKED SALMON

8 SERVINGS | 10 MINUTES | 3 HOURS

INSTRUCTIONS:

1. *Preheat your smoker to 225°F (107°C).*
2. *Mix maple syrup, soy sauce, and garlic powder in a bowl.*
3. *Brush the mixture over the salmon.*
4. *Smoke the salmon for about 3 hours.*
5. *Slice and serve.*

INGREDIENTS:

- 2 lbs salmon fillet (907 g)
- 1/4 cup maple syrup (60 ml)
- 2 tbsp soy sauce (30 ml)
- 1 tsp garlic powder (5 g)

NUTRITIONAL FACTS:

215 Kcal, 5g Cho, 7g Fat, 660mg Na, 23g Pro

CITRUS BRINED SMOKED SALMON

 8 SERVINGS

NUTRITIONAL FACTS:

180 Kcal, 0g Cho, 5g Fat, 1800mg Na, 27g Pro

 12 HOURS

 3 HOURS

INSTRUCTIONS:

1. Dissolve salt in water to make a brine.
2. Add orange and lemon juice along with zest.
3. Submerge salmon in the brine and refrigerate overnight.
4. Preheat smoker to 225°F (107°C).
5. Remove salmon from brine, pat dry.
6. Smoke for 3 hours.
7. Slice and serve.

INGREDIENTS:

- 2 lbs salmon fillet (907 g)
- 1/4 cup salt (60 g)
- 4 cups water (960 ml)
- 1 orange, juiced and zested (120 ml juice, 10 g zest)
- 1 lemon, juiced and zested (60 ml juice, 5 g zest)

ASIAN STYLE SMOKED SALMON

8 SERVINGS   10 MINUTES   3 HOURS

INSTRUCTIONS:

1. *Mix soy sauce, hoisin sauce, ginger, and garlic in a bowl.*
2. *Rub the mixture over the salmon.*
3. *Preheat your smoker to 225°F (107°C).*
4. *Place the salmon in the smoker.*
5. *Smoke for 3 hours.*
6. *Slice and serve.*

INGREDIENTS:

- 2 lbs salmon fillet (907 g)
- 1/4 cup soy sauce (60 ml)
- 2 tbsp hoisin sauce (30 ml)
- 2 tbsp ginger, minced (30 g)
- 2 cloves garlic, minced (8 g)

NUTRITIONAL FACTS:

205 Kcal, 5g Cho, 7g Fat, 670mg Na, 27g Pro

GRILLED SHRIMP DELIGHTS

GARLIC BUTTER GRILLED SHRIMP

8 SERVINGS   10 MINUTES   6 MINUTES

INSTRUCTIONS:

1. *Preheat grill to medium-high, about 375°F (190°C).*
2. *In a bowl, combine melted butter, garlic, lemon juice, parsley, salt, and pepper.*
3. *Toss the shrimp in the garlic butter mixture.*
4. *Thread shrimp onto skewers.*
5. *Grill for 3 minutes on each side or until shrimp are pink and cooked through.*
6. *Serve immediately.*

INGREDIENTS:

- 2 lbs shrimp, peeled and deveined (907 g)
- 1/4 cup butter, melted (60 ml)
- 4 cloves garlic, minced (16 g)
- 1 lemon, juiced (30 ml)
- 1 tbsp parsley, chopped (15 g)
- Salt and pepper to taste

NUTRITIONAL FACTS:

200 Kcal, 1g Cho, 8g Fat, 300mg Na, 24g Pro

SPICY GRILLED SHRIMP TACOS

 8 SERVINGS

 20 MINUTES

 6 MINUTES

NUTRITIONAL FACTS:

220 Kcal, 15g Cho, 10g Fat, 300mg Na, 20g Pro

INSTRUCTIONS:

1. Preheat grill to high, about 450°F (232°C).
2. Mix olive oil, chili powder, cumin, and garlic powder in a bowl.
3. Toss shrimp in the spice mixture.
4. Grill shrimp for 3 minutes on each side.
5. Assemble tacos using corn tortillas, grilled shrimp, avocado slices, and shredded cabbage.
6. Serve with lime wedges.

INGREDIENTS:

- 2 lbs shrimp, peeled and deveined (907 g)
- 2 tbsp olive oil (30 ml)
- 2 tsp chili powder (10 g)
- 1 tsp cumin (5 g)
- 1 tsp garlic powder (5 g)
- 8 corn tortillas (320 g)
- 1 avocado, sliced (200 g)
- 1 cup cabbage, shredded (70 g)
- Lime wedges for serving

CARIBBEAN JERK SHRIMP SKEWERS

8 SERVINGS   15 MINUTES   6 MINUTES

INSTRUCTIONS:

1. *Preheat grill to medium-high, about 375°F (190°C).*
2. *Toss shrimp with jerk seasoning and olive oil.*
3. *Thread shrimp and pineapple cubes alternately onto skewers.*
4. *Grill for 3 minutes on each side or until shrimp are pink and cooked through.*
5. *Serve skewers hot off the grill.*

INGREDIENTS:

- 2 lbs shrimp, peeled and deveined (907 g)
- 1/4 cup jerk seasoning (60 g)
- 2 tbsp olive oil (30 ml)
- 1 pineapple, cubed (450 g)

NUTRITIONAL FACTS:

210 Kcal, 10g Cho, 7g Fat, 880mg Na, 24g Pro

LEMON AND HERB SHRIMP FOIL PACKS

 8 SERVINGS

 10 MINUTES

 10 MINUTES

NUTRITIONAL FACTS:

195 Kcal, 3g Cho, 8g Fat, 300mg Na, 24g Pro

INSTRUCTIONS:

1. Preheat grill to medium, about 350°F (177°C).
2. Cut 8 sheets of foil.
3. Divide shrimp and lemon slices among the foil sheets.
4. Drizzle with olive oil and sprinkle with herbs, salt, and pepper.
5. Fold foil into packets.
6. Grill for 10 minutes or until shrimp are pink and cooked through.
7. Serve directly in the foil packets.

INGREDIENTS:

- 2 lbs shrimp, peeled and deveined (907 g)
- 2 lemons, sliced (100 g)
- 1/4 cup olive oil (60 ml)
- 1 tbsp mixed herbs (basil, parsley, thyme) (15 g)
- Salt and pepper to taste

THAI COCONUT CURRY SHRIMP

8 SERVINGS   15 MINUTES   10 MINUTES

INGREDIENTS:

- 2 lbs shrimp, peeled and deveined (907 g)
- 1 can coconut milk (400 ml)
- 2 tbsp Thai red curry paste (30 g)
- 1 tbsp fish sauce (15 ml)
- 1 tbsp sugar (15 g)
- 1 red bell pepper, sliced (150 g)
- 1/2 cup basil leaves, torn (15 g)

INSTRUCTIONS:

1. Preheat grill to medium-high, about 375°F (190°C).
2. In a large skillet on the grill, stir together coconut milk, curry paste, fish sauce, and sugar.
3. Add shrimp and bell pepper to the skillet.
4. Cook for about 8 minutes or until shrimp are cooked through.
5. Stir in basil leaves just before serving.
6. Serve hot, ideally over rice.

NUTRITIONAL FACTS:

280 Kcal, 5g Cho, 15g Fat, 400mg Na, 25g Pro

CREATIVE SEAFOOD MIXES

SMOKED CRAB CAKES

8 SERVINGS   20 MINUTES   30 MINUTES

INGREDIENTS:

- 1 lb crab meat, picked over for shells (453 g)
- 1 cup breadcrumbs (120 g)
- 1/4 cup mayonnaise (60 ml)
- 1 egg, beaten (50 g)
- 1 tbsp Dijon mustard (15 ml)
- 1 tbsp Worcestershire sauce (15 ml)
- 1/4 cup chopped parsley (15 g)
- Salt and pepper to taste

INSTRUCTIONS:

1. Mix crab meat, breadcrumbs, mayonnaise, egg, Dijon mustard, Worcestershire sauce, parsley, salt, and pepper in a bowl.
2. Form the mixture into 8 cakes.
3. Preheat smoker to 225°F (107°C).
4. Place crab cakes in the smoker.
5. Smoke for 30 minutes or until they are firm and cooked through.
6. Serve hot with lemon wedges.

NUTRITIONAL FACTS:

180 Kcal, 10g Cho, 8g Fat, 400mg Na, 17g Pro

GRILLED SCALLOPS WITH HERB BUTTER

  8 SERVINGS

  10 MINUTES

  6 MINUTES

NUTRITIONAL FACTS:

190 Kcal, 2g Cho, 8g Fat, 450mg Na, 27g Pro

INSTRUCTIONS:

1. Preheat grill to high, about 450°F (232°C).
2. Mix butter with garlic and herbs.
3. Season scallops with salt and pepper.
4. Grill scallops for 3 minutes on each side or until translucent.
5. Top each scallop with a dollop of herb butter just before serving.

INGREDIENTS:

- 2 lbs scallops (907 g)
- 1/4 cup butter, softened (60 ml)
- 1 tbsp chopped garlic (15 g)
- 2 tbsp chopped fresh herbs (parsley, chives) (30 g)
- Salt and pepper to taste

SMOKED LOBSTER TAILS WITH GARLIC BUTTER

8 SERVINGS   15 MINUTES   30 MINUTES

INGREDIENTS:

- 8 lobster tails (4 lbs or 1814 g)
- 1/2 cup butter, melted (120 ml)
- 4 cloves garlic, minced (16 g)
- 1 lemon, juiced (30 ml)
- Salt and pepper to taste

INSTRUCTIONS:

1. *Preheat smoker to 225°F (107°C).*
2. *Split lobster tails down the middle.*
3. *Mix butter with garlic, lemon juice, salt, and pepper.*
4. *Brush lobster tails with garlic butter.*
5. *Place lobster tails in the smoker.*
6. *Smoke for 30 minutes or until lobster meat is firm and opaque.*
7. *Serve immediately with extra garlic butter.*

NUTRITIONAL FACTS:

230 Kcal, og Cho, 15g Fat, 500mg Na, 23g Pro

CEDAR PLANK GRILLED TROUT

 8 SERVINGS

 10 MINUTES

 20 MINUTES

 NUTRITIONAL FACTS:

230 Kcal, og Cho, 15g Fat, 500mg Na, 23g Pro

INSTRUCTIONS:

1. Preheat smoker to 225°F (107°C).
2. Split lobster tails down the middle.
3. Mix butter with garlic, lemon juice, salt, and pepper.
4. Brush lobster tails with garlic butter.
5. Place lobster tails in the smoker.
6. Smoke for 30 minutes or until lobster meat is firm and opaque.
7. Serve immediately with extra garlic butter.

INGREDIENTS:

- 8 lobster tails (4 lbs or 1814 g)
- 1/2 cup butter, melted (120 ml)
- 4 cloves garlic, minced (16 g)
- 1 lemon, juiced (30 ml)
- Salt and pepper to taste

CEDAR PLANK GRILLED TROUT

8 SERVINGS   15 MINUTES   20 MINUTES

INGREDIENTS:

- 4 whole trout, cleaned (8 lbs or 3629 g)
- 2 lemons, sliced (100 g)
- 1/4 cup olive oil (60 ml)
- 2 tbsp fresh dill, chopped (30 g)
- Salt and pepper to taste
- 2 cedar planks (soaked in water for 2 hours)

INSTRUCTIONS:

1. *Preheat grill to medium, about 350°F (177°C).*
2. *Rub trout inside and out with olive oil, salt, and pepper.*
3. *Fill cavity of each trout with lemon slices and dill.*
4. *Place trout on soaked cedar planks.*
5. *Grill for 20 minutes or until fish flakes easily with a fork.*
6. *Serve directly from the cedar planks for added flavor.*

NUTRITIONAL FACTS:

340 Kcal, 0g Cho, 20g Fat, 380mg Na, 37g Pro

SMOKED CLAMS AND MUSSELS

   8 SERVINGS

  15 MINUTES

10 MINUTES

NUTRITIONAL FACTS:

200 Kcal, 5g Cho, 10g Fat, 580mg Na, 22g Pro

INGREDIENTS:

- 2 lbs clams, scrubbed (907 g)
- 2 lbs mussels, cleaned and debearded (907 g)
- 1/4 cup white wine (60 ml)
- 4 cloves garlic, minced (16 g)
- 1/4 cup chopped parsley (15 g)
- 2 tbsp butter (30 ml)

INSTRUCTIONS:

1. Preheat smoker to 250°F (121°C).
2. Place clams and mussels in a large disposable aluminum tray.
3. Add white wine, garlic, parsley, and dots of butter over the shellfish.
4. Cover tray with foil.
5. Smoke for 10 minutes or until all shells have opened.
6. Discard any that do not open.
7. Serve hot, garnished with additional parsley.

GRILLED CALAMARI WITH MEDITERRANEAN SALSA

8 SERVINGS   20 MINUTES   10 MINUTES

INSTRUCTIONS:

1. *Preheat grill to high, about 450°F (232°C).*
2. *Toss calamari with 1 tbsp olive oil, salt, and pepper.*
3. *Grill calamari for 2-3 minutes on each side until slightly charred and cooked through.*
4. *Combine tomatoes, cucumber, red onion, olives, feta, lemon juice, remaining olive oil, and parsley to make salsa.*
5. *Serve grilled calamari topped with Mediterranean salsa.*

INGREDIENTS:

- 2 lbs calamari, cleaned and tubes sliced into rings (907 g)
- 2 tomatoes, diced (200 g)
- 1 cucumber, diced (150 g)
- 1/4 cup red onion, finely chopped (40 g)
- 1/4 cup olives, chopped (30 g)
- 1/4 cup feta cheese, crumbled (60 g)
- 2 tbsp olive oil (30 ml)
- Juice of 1 lemon (30 ml)
- 1 tbsp parsley, chopped (15 g)
- Salt and pepper to taste

NUTRITIONAL FACTS:

180 Kcal, 5g Cho, 10g Fat, 380mg Na, 18g Pro

SMOKED OYSTERS WITH CHILI LIME BUTTER

 8 SERVINGS

 10 MINUTES

 10 MINUTES

NUTRITIONAL FACTS:

150 Kcal, 5g Cho, 12g Fat, 180mg Na, 10g Pro

INSTRUCTIONS:

1. Preheat smoker to 250°F (121°C).
2. Mix butter with chili powder, lime juice, and lime zest.
3. Place a dollop of chili lime butter on each oyster.
4. Smoke oysters for 10 minutes or until edges are slightly curled.
5. Serve hot

INGREDIENTS:

- 24 oysters, shucked (1200 g)
- 1/4 cup butter, softened (60 ml)
- 1 tbsp chili powder (15 g)
- 2 tbsp lime juice (30 ml)
- 1 tsp lime zest (5 g)

GRILLED OCTOPUS WITH OLIVE OIL AND LEMON

8 SERVINGS   10 MINUTES   10 MINUTES

INSTRUCTIONS:

1. *Preheat grill to medium-high, about 375°F (190°C).*
2. *Toss octopus tentacles with olive oil, lemon juice, garlic, salt, and pepper.*
3. *Grill octopus for 5 minutes on each side until charred and crispy.*
4. *Serve with additional lemon wedges.*

INGREDIENTS:

- 1 large octopus, pre-cooked and tentacles separated (3 lbs or 1360 g)
- 1/4 cup olive oil (60 ml)
- Juice of 1 lemon (30 ml)
- 2 cloves garlic, minced (8 g)
- Salt and pepper to taste
- Lemon wedges for serving

NUTRITIONAL FACTS:

250 Kcal, 0g Cho, 18g Fat, 470mg Na, 22g Pro

CAJUN STYLE GRILLED CATFISH

 8 SERVINGS

 10 MINUTES

 12 MINUTES

NUTRITIONAL FACTS:

220 Kcal, 0g Cho, 12g Fat, 580mg Na, 23g Pro

INSTRUCTIONS:

1. Preheat grill to medium, about 350°F (177°C).
2. Rub each catfish fillet with olive oil and Cajun seasoning.
3. Grill fillets for 6 minutes on each side or until the fish flakes easily with a fork.
4. Serve hot with lemon wedges.

INGREDIENTS:

- 4 catfish fillets (2 lbs or 907 g)
- 2 tbsp Cajun seasoning (30 g)
- 2 tbsp olive oil (30 ml)
- Lemon wedges for serving

SMOKED SEA BASS WITH CITRUS GLAZE

8 SERVINGS · 15 MINUTES · 20 MINUTES

INGREDIENTS:

- 2 lbs sea bass fillets (907 g)
- 1/4 cup orange juice (60 ml)
- 2 tbsp lemon juice (30 ml)
- 2 tbsp honey (30 ml)
- 1 tbsp soy sauce (15 ml)
- 2 tsp ginger, grated (10 g)
- Salt and pepper to taste

INSTRUCTIONS:

1. *Preheat smoker to 225°F (107°C).*
2. *Mix orange juice, lemon juice, honey, soy sauce, and ginger in a bowl.*
3. *Season sea bass with salt and pepper.*
4. *Brush fish with citrus glaze.*
5. *Smoke for 20 minutes, reapplying glaze halfway through.*
6. *Serve hot.*

NUTRITIONAL FACTS:

190 Kcal, 5g Cho, 7g Fat, 350mg Na, 23g Pro

GRILLED MAHI-MAHI WITH MANGO SALSA

 8 SERVINGS

 15 MINUTES

 10 MINUTES

 NUTRITIONAL FACTS:

240 Kcal, 10g Cho, 8g Fat, 150mg Na, 26g Pro

INGREDIENTS:

- 2 lbs Mahi-Mahi fillets (907 g)
- 2 mangoes, diced (300 g)
- 1 red bell pepper, diced (150 g)
- 1/2 red onion, finely chopped (75 g)
- 1/4 cup cilantro, chopped (15 g)
- Juice of 1 lime (30 ml)
- 2 tbsp olive oil (30 ml)
- Salt and pepper to taste

INSTRUCTIONS:

1. Preheat grill to high, about 450°F (232°C).
2. Brush Mahi-Mahi with olive oil, season with salt and pepper.
3. Grill fillets for 5 minutes on each side or until fish flakes easily with a fork.
4. Mix mangoes, red bell pepper, red onion, cilantro, and lime juice to make the salsa.
5. Serve grilled Mahi-Mahi topped with mango salsa.

SMOKED HADDOCK WITH CREAMY MUSTARD SAUCE

8 SERVINGS   10 MINUTES   20 MINUTES

INSTRUCTIONS:

1. *Preheat smoker to 225°F (107°C).*
2. *Brush haddock with olive oil, season with salt and pepper.*
3. *Smoke for 20 minutes or until cooked through.*
4. *Meanwhile, heat cream and Dijon mustard in a saucepan, stirring until thickened.*
5. *Stir in dill.*
6. *Serve smoked haddock with creamy mustard sauce.*

INGREDIENTS:

- 2 lbs haddock fillets (907 g)
- 1 cup cream (240 ml)
- 2 tbsp Dijon mustard (30 ml)
- 1 tbsp chopped dill (15 g)
- 1 tbsp olive oil (15 ml)
- Salt and pepper to taste

NUTRITIONAL FACTS:

210 Kcal, 2g Cho, 14g Fat, 180mg Na, 20g Pro

CARIBBEAN GRILLED LOBSTER WITH SPICED RUM

 8 SERVINGS

  20 MINUTES

 10 MINUTES

NUTRITIONAL FACTS:

330 Kcal, 1g Cho, 23g Fat, 560mg Na, 30g Pro

INSTRUCTIONS:

1. Preheat grill to medium, about 350°F (177°C).
2. Mix spiced rum, butter, brown sugar, allspice, salt, and pepper.
3. Brush mixture over lobster.
4. Grill lobsters, shell side down, for 5 minutes.
5. Flip and grill for another 5 minutes or until meat is opaque.
6. Serve hot.

INGREDIENTS:

- 4 whole lobsters, split (8 lbs or 3629 g)
- 1/4 cup spiced rum (60 ml)
- 1/4 cup butter, melted (60 ml)
- 2 tbsp brown sugar (30 g)
- 1 tsp allspice (5 g)
- Salt and pepper to taste

SMOKED WHITEFISH WITH DILL SAUCE

8 SERVINGS

10 MINUTES

90 MINUTES

INSTRUCTIONS:

1. *Preheat smoker to 225°F (107°C).*
2. *Brush whitefish with olive oil, season with salt and pepper.*
3. *Smoke for 90 minutes or until flaky.*
4. *Mix sour cream, dill, and lemon juice to make dill sauce.*
5. *Serve smoked whitefish with dill sauce.*

INGREDIENTS:

- 2 lbs whitefish fillets (907 g)
- 1 cup sour cream (240 ml)
- 1 tbsp fresh dill, chopped (15 g)
- 2 tsp lemon juice (10 ml)
- 1 tbsp olive oil (15 ml)
- Salt and pepper to taste

NUTRITIONAL FACTS:

210 Kcal, 2g Cho, 12g Fat, 110mg Na, 24g Pro

GRILLED SWORDFISH WITH CAPER BUTTER

8 SERVINGS

10 MINUTES

10 MINUTES

NUTRITIONAL FACTS:

INSTRUCTIONS:

1. Preheat grill to high, about 450°F (232°C).
2. Season swordfish with salt and pepper.
3. Grill for 5 minutes on each side or until cooked through.
4. Mix butter, capers, lemon juice, and parsley.
5. Serve swordfish steaks topped with caper butter.

INGREDIENTS:

- 2 lbs swordfish steaks (907 g)
- 1/4 cup butter, softened (60 ml)
- 2 tbsp capers, drained (30 g)
- 1 tbsp lemon juice (15 ml)
- 1 tbsp parsley, chopped (15 g)
- Salt and pepper to taste

CHAPTER 8: VEGETARIAN AND VEGAN DELIGHTS
TOFU AND TEMPEH SPECIALTIES

SMOKED TOFU WITH HOISIN GLAZE

8 SERVINGS   15 MINUTES   90 MINUTES

INSTRUCTIONS:

1. *Preheat smoker to 225°F (107°C).*
2. *Mix hoisin sauce, soy sauce, rice vinegar, garlic, and ginger in a bowl.*
3. *Brush tofu slices with the hoisin glaze.*
4. *Place tofu in the smoker and smoke for 1 hour 30 minutes, basting with glaze every 30 minutes.*
5. *Serve hot, garnished with green onions.*

INGREDIENTS:

- 2 lbs firm tofu, pressed and sliced (907 g)
- 1/2 cup hoisin sauce (120 ml)
- 2 tbsp soy sauce (30 ml)
- 2 tbsp rice vinegar (30 ml)
- 2 cloves garlic, minced (8 g)
- 1 tbsp ginger, grated (15 g)

NUTRITIONAL FACTS:

200 Kcal, 15g Cho, 10g Fat, 800mg Na, 12g Pro

GRILLED TEMPEH TACOS

 8 SERVINGS

 15 MINUTES

 10 MINUTES

NUTRITIONAL FACTS:

280 Kcal, 25g Cho, 12g Fat, 350mg Na, 15g Pro

INSTRUCTIONS:

1. Preheat grill to medium-high, about 375°F (190°C).
2. Toss tempeh strips with olive oil, chili powder, and cumin.
3. Grill tempeh for 5 minutes on each side.
4. Warm tortillas on the grill for 1 minute each side.
5. Assemble tacos with grilled tempeh, avocado, lettuce, and salsa.

INGREDIENTS:

- 2 lbs tempeh, sliced into strips (907 g)
- 2 tbsp olive oil (30 ml)
- 1 tbsp chili powder (15 g)
- 1 tsp cumin (5 g)
- 8 corn tortillas (320 g)
- 1 avocado, sliced (200 g)
- 1 cup shredded lettuce (50 g)
- 1/2 cup salsa (120 ml)

SMOKED TEMPEH WITH PINEAPPLE SALSA

8 SERVINGS   15 MINUTES   60 MINUTES

INSTRUCTIONS:

1. *Preheat smoker to 225°F (107°C).*
2. *Marinate tempeh slices in soy sauce and maple syrup for 10 minutes.*
3. *Smoke tempeh for 1 hour.*
4. *Combine pineapple, red bell pepper, red onion, cilantro, and lime juice to make salsa.*
5. *Serve smoked tempeh topped with pineapple salsa.*

INGREDIENTS:

- 2 lbs tempeh, sliced (907 g)
- 1/4 cup soy sauce (60 ml)
- 2 tbsp maple syrup (30 ml)
- 1 pineapple, diced (450 g)
- 1 red bell pepper, diced (150 g)
- 1/4 cup red onion, finely chopped (40 g)
- 1/4 cup cilantro, chopped (15 g)
- Juice of 1 lime (30 ml)

NUTRITIONAL FACTS:

250 Kcal, 25g Cho, 10g Fat, 800mg Na, 14g Pro

BBQ SMOKED TOFU SKEWERS

 8 SERVINGS

NUTRITIONAL FACTS:

230 Kcal, 12g Cho, 10g Fat, 700mg Na, 14g Pro

 20 MINUTES

 60 MINUTES

INSTRUCTIONS:

1. Preheat smoker to 225°F (107°C).
2. Toss tofu, peppers, and onion with olive oil, salt, and pepper.
3. Thread tofu and vegetables onto skewers.
4. Brush with BBQ sauce.
5. Smoke for 1 hour, basting with BBQ sauce halfway through.
6. Serve hot.

INGREDIENTS:

- 2 lbs firm tofu, cubed (907 g)
- 1/2 cup BBQ sauce (120 ml)
- 1 red bell pepper, cubed (150 g)
- 1 yellow bell pepper, cubed (150 g)
- 1 red onion, cubed (150 g)
- 2 tbsp olive oil (30 ml)
- Salt and pepper to taste

KOREAN BBQ TEMPEH

8 SERVINGS   15 MINUTES   10 MINUTES

INGREDIENTS:

- 2 lbs tempeh, sliced (907 g)
- 1/4 cup soy sauce (60 ml)
- 2 tbsp gochujang (30 g)
- 2 tbsp rice vinegar (30 ml)
- 2 tbsp brown sugar (30 g)
- 2 cloves garlic, minced (8 g)
- 1 tbsp ginger, grated (15 g)

INSTRUCTIONS:

1. *Preheat grill to medium-high, about 375°F (190°C).*
2. *Mix soy sauce, gochujang, rice vinegar, brown sugar, garlic, and ginger in a bowl.*
3. *Marinate tempeh slices in the mixture for 10 minutes.*
4. *Grill tempeh for 5 minutes on each side.*
5. *Serve hot with additional marinade on the side for dipping.*

NUTRITIONAL FACTS:

210 Kcal, 15g Cho, 8g Fat, 800mg Na, 15g Pro

VEGAN SMOKEHOUSE RECIPES

SMOKED VEGAN JERKY

8 SERVINGS   15 MINUTES   3 HOURS

INGREDIENTS:

- 2 cups textured vegetable protein (200 g)
- 1/2 cup soy sauce (120 ml)
- 2 tbsp maple syrup (30 ml)
- 1 tbsp liquid smoke (15 ml)
- 1 tbsp smoked paprika (15 g)
- 1 tsp garlic powder (5 g)
- 1 tsp onion powder (5 g)
- 1 tsp black pepper (5 g)

INSTRUCTIONS:

1. *Rehydrate textured vegetable protein in boiling water for 10 minutes.*
2. *Mix soy sauce, maple syrup, liquid smoke, smoked paprika, garlic powder, onion powder, and black pepper in a bowl.*
3. *Drain and press out excess water from the rehydrated TVP.*
4. *Marinate TVP in the soy sauce mixture for 30 minutes.*
5. *Preheat smoker to 200°F (93°C).*
6. *Place marinated TVP on smoker racks.*
7. *Smoke for 3 hours, flipping halfway through.*
8. *Let cool before serving.*

NUTRITIONAL FACTS:

120 Kcal, 10g Cho, 4g Fat, 890mg Na, 14g Pro

VEGAN SMOKED "PULLED PORK" FROM JACKFRUIT

  8 SERVINGS

 20 MINUTES

 2 HOURS

NUTRITIONAL FACTS:

180 Kcal, 20g Cho, 7g Fat, 400mg Na, 2g Pro

INSTRUCTIONS:

1. Shred jackfruit with a fork.
2. Mix BBQ sauce, olive oil, smoked paprika, garlic powder, onion powder, salt, and pepper in a bowl.
3. Toss jackfruit in the BBQ mixture.
4. Preheat smoker to 225°F (107°C).
5. Spread jackfruit on smoker racks.
6. Smoke for 2 hours, stirring occasionally.
7. Serve on buns or with your favorite sides.

INGREDIENTS:

- 2 cans young jackfruit, drained and rinsed (560 g)
- 1/4 cup BBQ sauce (60 ml)
- 2 tbsp olive oil (30 ml)
- 1 tbsp smoked paprika (15 g)
- 1 tsp garlic powder (5 g)
- 1 tsp onion powder (5 g)
- Salt and pepper to taste

SMOKED VEGAN CHEESE

8 SERVINGS   10 MINUTES   2 HOURS

INSTRUCTIONS:

1. *Drain and rinse soaked cashews.*
2. *Blend cashews with nutritional yeast, lemon juice, coconut oil, apple cider vinegar, miso paste, garlic powder, and salt until smooth.*
3. *Pour mixture into a cheese mold or small bowl lined with cheesecloth.*
4. *Refrigerate for 2 hours to set.*
5. *Preheat smoker to 225°F (107°C).*
6. *Place cheese in the smoker and smoke for 2 hours.*
7. *Let cool before serving.*

INGREDIENTS:

- 2 cups raw cashews, soaked overnight (300 g)
- 1/4 cup nutritional yeast (30 g)
- 1/4 cup lemon juice (60 ml)
- 2 tbsp coconut oil, melted (30 ml)
- 1 tbsp apple cider vinegar (15 ml)
- 1 tbsp miso paste (15 g)
- 1 tsp garlic powder (5 g)
- Salt to taste

NUTRITIONAL FACTS:

220 Kcal, 10g Cho, 16g Fat, 180mg Na, 7g Pro

SMOKED VEGAN CHILI

 8 SERVINGS

 15 MINUTES

 1 HOUR

NUTRITIONAL FACTS:

250 Kcal, 35g Cho, 8g Fat, 450mg Na, 10g Pro

INSTRUCTIONS:

1. Heat olive oil in a large pot over medium heat.
2. Sauté onion, bell pepper, and garlic until softened.
3. Add chili powder, smoked paprika, cumin, salt, and pepper; cook for 2 minutes.
4. Stir in kidney beans, diced tomatoes, and tomato sauce.
5. Simmer for 20 minutes.
6. Preheat smoker to 225°F (107°C).
7. Transfer chili to a smoker-safe dish.
8. Smoke for 1 hour.
9. Serve hot.

INGREDIENTS:

- 2 cups cooked kidney beans (400 g)
- 1 cup diced tomatoes (240 g)
- 1 cup tomato sauce (240 ml)
- 1 onion, diced (150 g)
- 1 bell pepper, diced (150 g)
- 2 cloves garlic, minced (8 g)
- 1 tbsp chili powder (15 g)
- 1 tsp smoked paprika (5 g)
- 1 tsp cumin (5 g)
- 2 tbsp olive oil (30 ml)
- Salt and pepper to taste

SMOKED VEGAN MEATBALLS

8 SERVINGS

20 MINUTES

1 HOUR

INSTRUCTIONS:

1. Preheat smoker to 225°F (107°C).
2. Mix flaxseed meal and water; let sit for 5 minutes.
3. Combine lentils, breadcrumbs, onions, garlic, nutritional yeast, flax mixture, soy sauce, smoked paprika, salt, and pepper.
4. Form into meatballs and place on smoker racks.
5. Smoke for 1 hour.
6. Serve with your favorite sauce.

INGREDIENTS:

- 2 cups cooked lentils (400 g)
- 1 cup breadcrumbs (120 g)
- 1/2 cup chopped onions (75 g)
- 2 cloves garlic, minced (8 g)
- 1/4 cup nutritional yeast (30 g)
- 2 tbsp flaxseed meal mixed with 6 tbsp water (30 g + 90 ml)
- 1 tbsp soy sauce (15 ml)
- 1 tsp smoked paprika (5 g)
- Salt and pepper to taste

NUTRITIONAL FACTS:

180 Kcal, 25g Cho, 5g Fat, 300mg Na, 8g Pro

CHAPTER 9: THE SWEETER SIDE
DESSERTS ON A GRILL

GRILLED PINEAPPLE WITH CINNAMON SUGAR

8 SERVINGS

5 MINUTES

10 MINUTES

INSTRUCTIONS:

1. *Preheat grill to medium-high, about 375°F (190°C).*
2. *Mix sugar and cinnamon in a small bowl.*
3. *Sprinkle cinnamon sugar over pineapple rings.*
4. *Grill pineapple rings for 5 minutes on each side until caramelized and grill marks appear.*
5. *Serve warm.*

INGREDIENTS:

- 1 whole pineapple, peeled, cored, and cut into rings (1 kg)
- 1/4 cup sugar (55 g)
- 1 tbsp cinnamon (15 g)

NUTRITIONAL FACTS:

100 Kcal, 25g Cho, 0g Fat, 2mg Na, 1g Pro

SMOKED CHOCOLATE BROWNIES

8 SERVINGS

10 MINUTES

1 HOUR

NUTRITIONAL FACTS:

270 Kcal, 38g Cho, 12g Fat, 80mg Na, 4g Pro

INSTRUCTIONS:

1. Preheat smoker to 225°F (107°C).
2. Whisk together sugar, melted butter, eggs, and vanilla.
3. Stir in cocoa, flour, salt, and baking powder.
4. Pour batter into a greased baking pan.
5. Place pan in the smoker and smoke for 1 hour.
6. Allow to cool before slicing.

INGREDIENTS:

- 1 cup sugar (200 g)
- 1/2 cup unsalted butter, melted (120 ml)
- 2 eggs (100 g)
- 1 tsp vanilla extract (5 ml)
- 1/3 cup unsweetened cocoa powder (40 g)
- 1/2 cup flour (60 g)
- 1/4 tsp salt (1.25 g)
- 1/4 tsp baking powder (1.25 g)

GRILLED PEACHES WITH HONEY AND CREAM

8 SERVINGS   5 MINUTES   10 MINUTES

INGREDIENTS:

- 4 peaches, halved and pitted (500 g)
- 1/4 cup honey (60 ml)
- 1 cup heavy cream, whipped (240 ml)

INSTRUCTIONS:

1. *Preheat grill to medium, about 350°F (177°C).*
2. *Brush peach halves with honey.*
3. *Grill peaches, cut side down, for 5 minutes.*
4. *Flip and grill for another 5 minutes until tender.*
5. *Serve with a dollop of whipped cream.*

NUTRITIONAL FACTS:

160 Kcal, 20g Cho, 10g Fat, 20mg Na, 2g Pro

SMOKED APPLE CRISP

  8 SERVINGS

NUTRITIONAL FACTS:

290 Kcal, 45g Cho, 12g Fat, 5mg Na, 3g Pro

  15 MINUTES

  90 MINUTES

INSTRUCTIONS:

1. Preheat smoker to 225°F (107°C).
2. In a large bowl, toss apples with brown sugar and cinnamon.
3. In another bowl, mix oats, flour, and butter until crumbly.
4. Layer apples in a baking dish and top with the oat mixture.
5. Smoke for 1 hour 30 minutes.
6. Serve warm.

INGREDIENTS:

- 6 apples, peeled, cored, and sliced (900 g)
- 1/2 cup brown sugar (100 g)
- 1 cup oats (90 g)
- 1/2 cup flour (60 g)
- 1/2 cup unsalted butter, cubed (120 g)
- 1 tsp cinnamon (5 g)

GRILLED BANANA BOATS

8 SERVINGS   5 MINUTES   10 MINUTES

INGREDIENTS:

- 8 bananas, unpeeled, slit lengthwise (1200 g)
- 1/2 cup chocolate chips (90 g)
- 1/2 cup mini marshmallows (50 g)
- 1/4 cup peanut butter (60 ml)

INSTRUCTIONS:

1. *Preheat grill to medium, about 350°F (177°C).*
2. *Stuff each banana with chocolate chips, marshmallows, and a spoonful of peanut butter.*
3. *Wrap bananas in foil.*
4. *Grill for 10 minutes, turning occasionally.*
5. *Carefully unwrap and serve warm.*

NUTRITIONAL FACTS:

230 Kcal, 40g Cho, 8g Fat, 60mg Na, 3g Pro

BAKING WITH YOUR TRAEGER

SMOKED CARROT CAKE

8 SERVINGS   20 MINUTES   2 HOURS

INGREDIENTS:

- 2 cups all-purpose flour (240 g)
- 1 1/2 cups sugar (300 g)
- 1 tsp baking powder (5 g)
- 1/2 tsp baking soda (2.5 g)
- 1 tsp cinnamon (5 g)
- 1/2 tsp salt (2.5 g)
- 1 cup vegetable oil (240 ml)
- 4 eggs (200 g)
- 2 cups grated carrots (200 g)
- 1 cup crushed pineapple, drained (225 g)

INSTRUCTIONS:

1. *Preheat smoker to 250°F (121°C).*
2. *In a large bowl, mix flour, sugar, baking powder, baking soda, cinnamon, and salt.*
3. *Stir in oil and eggs until smooth.*
4. *Fold in carrots and pineapple.*
5. *Pour batter into a greased baking pan.*
6. *Smoke for 2 hours or until a toothpick inserted comes out clean.*
7. *Allow to cool and frost if desired.*

NUTRITIONAL FACTS:

520 Kcal, 70g Cho, 25g Fat, 300mg Na, 7g Pro

GRILLED S'MORES

        8 SERVINGS

        5 MINUTES

        5 MINUTES

INGREDIENTS:

- 8 graham crackers, halved (120 g)
- 4 bars milk chocolate (200 g)
- 8 large marshmallows (100 g)

NUTRITIONAL FACTS:

300 Kcal, 45g Cho, 15g Fat, 150mg Na, 3g Pro

INSTRUCTIONS:

1. Preheat grill to medium, about 350°F (177°C).
2. Place one square of chocolate on one half of each graham cracker.
3. Skewer marshmallows and grill until browned, rotating constantly.
4. Place a grilled marshmallow on top of each chocolate piece.
5. Top with the other graham cracker half, pressing down gently.6. Serve immediately while warm and gooey.

SMOKED LEMON POUND CAKE

 8 SERVINGS

 15 MINUTES

 90 MINUTES

INSTRUCTIONS:

1. *Preheat smoker to 325°F (163°C).*
2. *Cream together sugar and butter until fluffy.*
3. *Add eggs, sour cream, lemon zest, and lemon juice, mixing well.*
4. *Gradually add flour and baking powder, mixing until smooth.*
5. *Pour batter into a greased loaf pan.*
6. *Smoke for 1 hour 30 minutes or until a toothpick inserted in the center comes out clean.*
7. *Let cool before slicing.*

INGREDIENTS:

- 1 1/2 cups sugar (300 g)
- 1 cup butter, softened (240 g)
- 4 eggs (200 g)
- 1/2 cup sour cream (120 ml)
- 2 tbsp lemon zest (30 g)
- 1/4 cup lemon juice (60 ml)
- 2 cups all-purpose flour (240 g)
- 1 tsp baking powder (5 g)

NUTRITIONAL FACTS:

460 Kcal, 60g Cho, 22g Fat, 150mg Na, 6g Pro

GRILLED CHEESECAKE

 8 SERVINGS

 10 MINUTES

 30 MINUTES

NUTRITIONAL FACTS:

350 Kcal, 20g Cho, 25g Fat, 200mg Na, 6g Pro

INSTRUCTIONS:

1. Preheat grill to 325°F (163°C) with indirect heat.
2. Beat cream cheese and sugar until smooth.
3. Add eggs and vanilla, mixing thoroughly.
4. Stir in sour cream.
5. Pour filling into graham cracker crust.
6. Place on grill away from direct heat and cover.
7. Grill for 30 minutes or until set.
8. Let cool and refrigerate before serving.

INGREDIENTS:

- 2 cups cream cheese, softened (480 g)
- 1/2 cup sugar (100 g)
- 2 eggs (100 g)
- 1 tsp vanilla extract (5 ml)
- 1/2 cup sour cream (120 ml)
- 1 graham cracker crust (pre-made) (150 g)

SMOKED BANANA BREAD

8 SERVINGS

20 MINUTES

2 HOURS

INSTRUCTIONS:

1. *Preheat smoker to 325°F (163°C).*
2. *Combine bananas, sugar, butter, eggs, and vanilla in a bowl.*
3. *Add flour, baking soda, and salt, mixing until just combined.*
4. *Pour batter into a greased loaf pan.*
5. *Smoke for 1 hour or until a toothpick inserted into the center comes out clean.*
6. *Let cool before slicing.*

INGREDIENTS:

- 3 ripe bananas, mashed (300 g)
- 3/4 cup sugar (150 g)
- 1/2 cup melted butter (120 ml)
- 2 eggs (100 g)
- 1 tsp vanilla extract (5 ml)
- 1 1/2 cups all-purpose flour (180 g)
- 1 tsp baking soda (5 g)
- 1/2 tsp salt (2.5 g)

NUTRITIONAL FACTS:

330 Kcal, 50g Cho, 15g Fat, 300mg Na, 4g Pro

CONCLUSION

BRINGING IT ALL TOGETHER

As we close this comprehensive guide on mastering the Traeger grill, it's evident that what started as basic grilling instruction has transformed into a rich culinary adventure. Each chapter has not only equipped you with the necessary skills to operate and maintain your grill but has also expanded your culinary repertoire, showcasing the unique flavors and techniques that wood-fired cooking offers.

Grilling on a Traeger is more than a cooking method; it's a commitment to a lifestyle that prizes quality, creativity, and community. From perfectly smoked meats to unexpected treats like desserts, you've learned to make each meal an occasion. The Traeger grill is not just a tool but a gateway to exploring new culinary landscapes and bringing people together over delicious food.

You now understand how to leverage the versatility of your grill for both large celebrations and quiet family dinners. By embracing the slow cooking process required for an impeccable BBQ, you've gained an appreciation for the nuances of flavor and the joy of sharing these creations with others.

Although this book marks a milestone in your grilling education, your evolution as a Traeger chef is just beginning. To further refine your skills and expand your cooking horizons, consider the following avenues for growth:

1.   Experiment with New Recipes: Keep challenging yourself with new recipes and techniques. Every ingredient offers a chance to innovate and create diverse dishes on your Traeger grill. Delve into international cuisines and bring global flavors to your backyard.

2.   Join Communities: Engage with fellow Traeger enthusiasts through online platforms, social media groups, or local meet-ups. These communities are treasure troves of knowledge, offering new recipes, tips, and the camaraderie of shared experiences.

3.   Take Classes: Enroll in workshops or classes that focus on smoking and grilling. Learning from seasoned experts can introduce you to advanced techniques and inspire new approaches to your grilling.

4.   Teach Others: Share your skills and knowledge by teaching friends or family. Hosting cooking demonstrations or informal grill sessions cements your knowledge and spreads the joy of grilling.

5.   Stay Updated: Keep abreast of the latest in Traeger technology and culinary trends. Manufacturers frequently introduce new features and accessories that can enhance your grilling experience.

6.   Document Your Culinary Adventures: Maintain a grilling journal to track your recipes, pellet choices, temperature settings, and timings. This record can be an invaluable tool for refining your techniques and inspiring future creations.

y continually seeking out new experiences and knowledge, you ensure that your growth s a Traeger chef never stagnates. Remember, the key to mastery lies in the ongoing ursuit of excellence and the enjoyment of the journey. With your Traeger grill by your ide, each meal becomes an opportunity to explore, create, and delight. Keep your passion or grilling alive, and enjoy every moment of this delicious adventure. Happy grilling!

GRATITUDE

s I pen down the final lines of this book, my heart is full of gratitude. This deep exploration nto the world of Traeger grilling has been more than just an exercise in writing; it has een a profound personal and professional endeavor. Writing this book allowed me to onnect with so many individuals, from family and friends who endured endless taste ests to professionals who shared their in-depth knowledge and enthusiasts who were nspired by their passion.

irst, I must thank my family, who have been incredibly supportive throughout the process. hey endured numerous weekend barbecues and provided honest feedback, which was rucial. Their patience and encouragement have been the bedrock of this project.

o the team at Traeger, whose support was invaluable. Your willingness to answer technical uestions and provide insights into the subtleties of your grills helped ensure the accuracy nd depth of the information presented.

special thanks goes to the culinary experts and chefs who generously shared their time nd expertise. Your innovative techniques and recipes have been a beacon for this guide, roviding it with the flavor and flair that I hope will inspire many.

o my friends and the broader Traeger community online, your enthusiasm and stories ave been incredibly motivating. This book is not just mine; it is a compilation of all your xperiences and shared love for grilling.

FINAL THOUGHTS

Vriting this book has been a transformative experience. The more I delved into the art nd science of Traeger grilling, the more I discovered about the nuances that make this tyle of cooking special. Each recipe tested and each technique mastered told a story of radition melded with innovation.

or those of you who pick up this book, whether you are novices hoping to learn about raeger grilling or seasoned grill masters looking to expand your repertoire, I hope it erves as a trusted resource.

More than that, I hope it inspires you to create your own recipes and traditions, to gathe friends and family around the grill, and to share in the joy of cooking together.

The world of Traeger grilling is vast and varied. As you continue to explore and experimen remember that every mistake is a lesson learned and every success a moment to savo Keep your grill hot, your pantry stocked, and your mind open to the endless possibilitie that await.

To all future grillers, may your food always be flavorful, your company joyful, and you grilling adventures exciting. Thank you for sharing this path with me. May the smoke fron your Traeger grill carry the promise of delicious meals and great memories.

Now, as you close this book, don't see it as the end. Instead, see it as an invitation to ligh up your grill, to try something new, and to make every meal an occasion. Happy grilling and may your culinary adventures be many and memorable.

Made in the USA
Las Vegas, NV
08 December 2024

13599343R00063